PRINCIPLES to REPOSITION

By
LaFlower Bowie

www.selfpublishn30days.com

Published by *Self Publish -N- 30 Days*

Copyright 2019 LaFlower Bowie.

All rights reserved worldwide. No part of this book may be reproduced or transmitted in any form or by any means electronic or mechanical, including photocopying, recording or by any information storage and retrieval system without written permission from LaFlower Bowie.

Printed in the United States of America

ISBN: 978-1687557254

1. Inspiration 2. Self Help

LaFlower Bowie.

PRINCIPLES to REPOSITION

Disclaimer/Warning:

This book is intended for lecture and entertainment purposes only. The author or publisher does not guarantee that anyone following these steps will be successful in life. The author and publisher shall have neither liability responsibility to anyone with respect to any loss or damage cause, or alleged to be caused, directly or indirectly by the information contained in this book.

DEDICATION

To my late father, Clifton Earl Virgil, Sr.:
Thank you for unapologetically being you.
I am grateful for the love, memories and life lessons.

Love always,

Little Momma
#GAHAAW

To my husband, Marcus:
Words cannot express my appreciation for all that you do. You loved me even when I didn't love myself. You saw the best version of me even when I couldn't see past my flaws. Your love and support continues to encourage me to never settle and always take it to the next level. Thank you. 143b

To my mother, sisters and brother:
Thank you, guys, for your continuous love and support.

To my children:
Thank you for making me better. Thank you for filling my heart with so much love and joy. I am proud and honored to be your mother.

TABLE OF CONTENTS

Introduction 1

Chapter 1   His Presence on My Life..3

Chapter 2   Trust His Word 9

Chapter 3   Christ Within You..15

Chapter 4   Praise & Worship...21

Chapter 5   Intimacy Through Fasting, Prayer & Giving...........25

Chapter 6   The Reason for the Lie 33

Chapter 7   Self-Care..39

Chapter 8   Promises Renewed 43

Chapter 9   Gratitude & Reflection...49

Consistency Chain 90-Day Challenge..53

INTRODUCTION

Wow, I cannot believe that all of this has happened. The journey, it seems so short. Thinking back to December 2015, I was in a state of unworthiness, self-doubt and sadness. I was unhappy and merely existing. I lay in bed grieving the loss of the woman who my soul yearned to be.

Today, everything is different. I am so excited that I decided to fight like hell to find my purpose, to understand my purpose and to live a purpose-driven life. Some may say that I was tripping. Some will say that I was just doing too much. We all have defining moments in our lives. Moments that allow us to see the current state of our individual journey, without filters, nor secondary opinion. Moments like this give us the opportunity to get MAD and make a decision to do something that will change the trajectory of our future.

During this time, I started to listen to my own voice and I began spending time alone. For people looking from the outside in, it appeared as if I was taking a few steps back because there was no progression in a physical sense. I knew that in order for me to live the purpose-driven life that God ordained for me, I had to make a decision to find the voice inside of me and grow spiritually.

I can clearly understand that the adversary fights so hard to keep us from understanding what is ours by divine purpose and right. No longer will I settle for a life of mediocrity. No longer will I settle for being complacent. Never again will I look at that Proverbs 31 woman and say that she is a mere example and that there is no way that a woman in today's time can live that kind of life and still function in life.

Principles to Reposition was birthed from a place of such deep pain and internal chaos. Yet God is so amazing how he will turn our complete mess and messiness into beauty, gold and diamonds. Just when I thought that I was at my breaking point, he was there.

I am even more grateful that I did not have to go through this alone. For the help from my family, friends, children and my husband I am forever grateful. Being surrounded by a tribe of people who acknowledge and appreciate who you are in the natural and spiritual has helped me embrace my divine purpose.

I pray that this book ignites a fire in everyone who reads it and that this fire will lead you to the answers that you have been seeking. I pray that this fire within you will challenge you to be the best version of you and that the fire is so strong that you can no longer live a life of comfort and complacency. I pray that this book refuels or re-ignites a fire within that may have been turned down low or blown out by hurt, pain, doubt, abuse, anxiety and fear. This new fresh fire will be one that nothing and no one can take away from you.

As you read this book, take what speaks to you and apply the tools to your circumstances and life in order to help you along your journey of purpose. This book is a seed and I declare it will bring in a harvest for the Kingdom through your faith. Amen.

Chapter 1

His Presence on My Life

I remember the first time I wanted to receive more of God. I was 15 years old, standing on the side of my parents' home facing the back yard. My parents wanted more of God as well, so my mother fully transitioned us from our family's traditional Baptist church to a "Holiness Church," and my father was waiting to hear from God regarding our permanent place of fellowship.

While attending our new church, **I began to see God through a new lens**, one that enabled us to speak in different tongues and cast out demonic spirits. I saw people praising God freely, not caring about how they looked or sounded to those around them. One time a prophetess at the church told me that I was anointed. This really encouraged me to want to know God more even though I didn't fully understand what she meant or about the anointing. I wanted what I saw the others had.

So, as I stood near the backyard looking up at the sky, I said to God, "I want to speak in tongues because I want more of you." Day after day I would go to the same spot near the backyard and pray.

I'm not sure how I expected it to happen, that I would suddenly be speaking in tongues, but I liked being there with God. I practiced, for lack of a better word, trying to decrease my own thoughts while praying and making what some may call babbling baby noises. I continued because I felt the Spirit of God. Once I received my heavenly language, I was amazed that I was able to have such an

I BEGAN TO SEE GOD THROUGH A NEW LENS

— ★ ★ ★ —

intimate connection with the Most High God. Here I was, just some little girl from the country who appeared to be invisible to most people most of the time, having this very real and very special connection with the true, living, real God. How could my life ever be the same?

A few months later, my understanding of God went even deeper as a woman of God prophesied to me at church in front of my mom. She told me that I had asked for my heavenly language and that I had received it because God heard me loud and clear. In that moment, I felt myself going deeper in God.

My love for God increased when he showed his love to me through that woman of God. When God speaks directly to you through another person, no matter the message, you think, "Wow, God does know me and he does see me. He does love me. He spoke to me." He will also speak directly to us if only we will listen. Growing up as a middle child can leave you feeling left out or even forgotten about, but at that moment God's love made me feel like I was an only child. I understood that he doesn't have to part the sky and speak to me in some mystical, low, slow, deep voice that can be portrayed in some TV shows or movies. God can, and will, use people, places and things to communicate with people.

I was excited for my new relationship and learning with God and for my future. However, it seemed that as time went by, my focus on the things of the world became greater than my focus on the things of God. I had what I call a roller-coaster relationship with God. I thought that the reason my life seemed like a roller-coaster ride was because he was taking me through the process of becoming the woman that he wanted me be. But one day I realized that HE NEVER changed. Hebrews 13:8 says, "Jesus Christ is the same yesterday and today and forever."

Everything in life changes. Relationships definitely change. Each event or circumstance that comes our way gives us the opportunity to choose growth and change. Some people grow and change for the better and some don't at all.

Many times people just grow apart because they want different things or think differently. Some differences will be so critical that the relationship must end.

However, God's love and commitment towards me is never based on my performance or how good I think I am or how much I do to please him. God will not change his mind about me because I am not perfect. This can be a huge revelation to people and can set many free from chasing after something we already have. God knew me before I was in my mother's womb. He already knew all of my shortcomings, fears and desires. He never changes toward me.

In fact, God was never even on the roller coaster with me. I was on the roller coaster with myself. I was always trying to find balance and clarity between the reality of who I was, who I longed to be and the LaFlower that others wanted me to be. But just like an earthly father, God was waiting on me at the bottom of the roller coaster the entire time. All along he was waiting patiently for me to simply receive him as the God of all Gods, the King of Kings, the Most High God.

As I was on this roller coaster ride, I dealt with all my sins and then I dealt with financial disciplines. I moved on to deal with my lusts. I dealt with church hurt. I dealt with resentment. I dealt with my insecurities. Should I go on? I dealt with feelings of being unworthy. I dealt with resentment towards my parents. I dealt with being a teenage mother. Oh, God, does it never end? I dealt with being a single mother. I dealt with being taken advantage of sexually by a man. And I dealt with false idols (aka men, just to name a few).

EVERYTHING IN LIFE CHANGES

— ★ ★ ★ —

The key word here is "I" dealt with it. Even as I type this I am exhausted from all this "dealing with myself" I had going on. Somewhere I must have missed the day Jesus said, "It is finished." The cross took care of everything and here I was trying to do it all myself. It's already been done. Does this sound familiar? So often we think it's up to us to clean ourselves up for God. Jesus has that all covered.

To add to my "fixing me," every now and then I would do what most Christians do. I would consult with God over all that I was dealing with and expect him to tell me what I should do next. Or, when I felt the need, I would cry out in my agony and pray for God to intervene. I never realized that I created the majority of the twists and turns on that roller coaster all because I was only consulting with God. I was not being led by God. There is a huge difference.

Consulting with God is when we acknowledge an issue and only pray and talk to God about it when we feel it is needed. Or perhaps, we may even apply a few Scriptures here and there, as if applying a Bandaid over it. However, when we are led by God, we take everything to the King. It doesn't matter how big or small, and we apply the full, unchangeable Word of God to every situation and detail in our lives. We do it continually, not just sometimes or when we are desperate.

Regardless of Popular Opinion

While doing a spiritual checkup, I asked myself if I really believed Genesis 1:1, "In the beginning God created the heavens and the earth." I then told myself, "If you really believed this, then you would take God off the dusty shelf and tear up that small box that you have kept him in all these years." Regardless of popular opinion, knowing God and having a thirst for him is needed now more than ever before.

I WAS NOT BEING LED BY GOD

— ★ ★ ★ —

I am sure that you have heard many believers say that we are living in the last days. I can honestly say that I have heard this since I was a little girl sitting on the pews of my grandfather's church in the country. But look around and see how the darkness is increasing and yet the light, which should be increasing, is not. Now that my spiritual eyes have been opened, I see a lot of so-called spiritual people walking the earth, but only a small percentage seem to actually be serving the Most High God. There are many who have a form of godliness displayed in their spirituality and how they live, but having a form of godliness does not always equate to a pursuit of righteousness.

"But seek first the kingdom of God and His righteousness"
Matthew 6:33a

"…having a form of godliness but denying its power…"
2 Timothy 3:5a

We have adopted this instant gratification mindset and have become self-proclaimed scholars who think we have mastered a deep belief system, yet we lack substance. This lack is evident in our need to challenge anything that, or anyone who, goes against our worldly desires, needs and fears by saying "We are gods. We are God. I choose the path for MY life."

In choosing this path, so many have traded in their seat in the pews to become full or part-time members of YouTube African Methodist Episcopal Church and Streaming Faith Missionary Baptist Church. Now, there is nothing wrong with getting a Word from those sources. Why do so many refuse to see the truth of Hebrews 10:24-25?

> "And let us consider one another in order to stir up love and good works, not forsaking the assembling of ourselves together, as *is* the manner of some, but exhorting *one another*, and so much the more as you see the Day approaching."

From personal experience, I truly believe that the voltage of the experience is ten times greater when you are assembled with other believers sending up timber and praises together with one accord.

Let's compare it to a phone being charged with a super charger verses a generic one. Everyone knows that no matter how low the battery is, no matter how many apps are running, once you connect to the super charger, that device will be back to 100% in no time. This allows you to not miss a beat while feeling secure because you know that you have a reliable lifeline to get help at any time. Now I know we have all had a janky cord or two that wouldn't charge our phone. Or we had to hold it in a certain position, leaving us uncertain if the phone would be charged overnight.

WE TAKE EVERYTHING TO THE KING

It may sound like a strange analogy, but the same thing goes for our relationship and having a strong connection with God. We shouldn't want our connection with God to be diluted or janky. Let us not forget that we have an enemy who is aiming to steal, kill and destroy us and our lives. He is playing in the major leagues and he is fully charged and ready to keep you from being the most powerful, fully charged man or woman of God you were destined to be.

I am on a mission to reconnect people to the ultimate power source because I am tired of seeing so many powerless believers losing a fight they have already won.

Chapter 2

Trust His Word

I consider myself to be an avid reader and I must say that the Bible has been the best book that I have ever read in my life. It is filled with supernatural events, drama, lies, love, beauty, joy, abundance and the real undisputed G.O.A.T - Jesus. As one opens the Bible and begins reading in Genesis, a few of the wonders of greatness are revealed as the author, Moses, shares with us about the creation process.

While preparing to write this chapter, I struggled to find provoking words to expand your mind in a spiritual capacity so you can have a glimpse of the fullness of God and his truth.

As I began to write, one of my all-time favorite worship songs came on. The melody is great, but the words ring a resounding truth throughout my body, soul and spirit. Tears began to pour down my face while reading the lyrics. I had finally encountered a piece of work that not only describes God, but also where the writer was able to lyrically describe how a believer may feel once they have been enlightened and fully surrendered.

I challenge you to not only read the words below, but also download the song and allow the Holy Spirit to move in and over you as you worship.

So Will I (100 Billion X)

Hillsong United

God of creation
There at the start
Before the beginning of time
With no point of reference
You spoke to the dark
And fleshed out the wonder of light
And as You speak
A hundred billion galaxies are born
In the vapor of Your breath the planets form
If the stars were made to worship, so will I
I can see Your heart in everything You've made
Every burning star
A signal fire of grace
If creation sings Your praises, so will I
God of Your promise
You don't speak in vain
No syllable empty or void
For once You have spoken
All nature and science
Follow the sound of Your voice
And as You speak
A hundred billion creatures catch Your breath
Evolving in pursuit of what You said
If it all reveals Your nature, so will I
I can see Your heart in everything You say
Every painted sky
A canvas of Your grace
If creation still obeys You, so will I
So will I

2. Trust His Word

So will I
If the stars were made to worship, so will I
If the mountains bow in reverence, so will I
If the oceans roar Your greatness, so will I
For if everything exists to lift You high, so will I
If the wind goes where You send it, so will I
If the rocks cry out in silence, so will I
If the sum of all our praises still falls shy
Then we'll sing again a hundred billion times
God of salvation
You chased down my heart
Through all of my failure and pride
On a hill You created
The light of the world
Abandoned in darkness to die
And as You speak
A hundred billion failures disappear
Where You lost Your life so I could find it here
If You left the grave behind You, so will I
I can see Your heart in everything You've done
Every part designed in a work of art called love
If You gladly chose surrender, so will I
I can see Your heart
Eight billion different ways
Every precious one
A child You died to save
If You gave Your life to love them, so will I
Like You would again a hundred billion times
But what measure could amount to Your desire
You're the One who never leaves the one behind

> **IF THE STARS WERE MADE TO WORSHIP, SO WILL I**
>
> — ★ ★ ★ —

While listening to the song, I began to flash back to some instances in my life in which I know I was the <u>one who he would never leave behind.</u> I have shed many tears thinking about the pain, sorrow and abandonment that I felt when my earthly father was killed. On the day of the accident, he decided to go to work to make some extra money for an upcoming trip that I had to Washington D.C. So one can only imagine the guilt and hurt that I carried for many years because I thought that he would still be here if it wasn't for me.

The song "So Will I" ministers to me because it reminds me that God is so BIG and nothing happens unless he allows it because he is that big. Even though I lost my earthly father at the age of 17, my heavenly father has always and will always be there.

No Escape

While working as a telecommunications technician in a nice suburban neighborhood in the Houston metro area, my faith was tested like never before. I had been with the company for some years and enjoyed my job. I liked not having to be in a restricted office all day. Plus, every day was an adventure because I got to meet new people and problem solve.

The day started just like any other day and I was pretty happy that my first home installation was an apartment in a nice area. Upon arriving at the customer's residence, I started on the installation the same way I always did. While working inside of the networking panel located in the guest room closet, I began to hear some other voices that sounded very aggressive. Something did not feel right, so I tried to call my manager and boyfriend, but there was no cellular signal. Looking around the closet and guest room, I realized that there was no escape and nowhere to hide.

Before I knew it, the voices got louder and I heard a man say, "Where is that technician B**** at?" Instead of having him find me, I slowly walked out of the closet saying, "Here I am."

There were two men with guns screaming at me, "Don't look at me! I am going to shoot you, if you look at me". I was directed to get on my knees, execution style, next to the customer and his girlfriend while the men raided the apartment. Once they were done, I was placed in the bathtub with the girlfriend. The young girl started screaming and cursing. I took a few deep breaths then started praying with the Our Father's prayer. The young girl appeared to be annoyed and asked why I was praying. I responded, "If I am going to die here, I want to die talking to my heavenly Father."

Sometime later, the bathroom door opened and it was the police. I knew without a shadow of a doubt that I made it out of that bathroom alive because I was covered and protected, just as God promised he would.

Needless to say, this was a traumatic event in my life and I was grateful to be able to take a leave of absence from work in order to heal and recover from the trauma. When it was time to return to work, I did, but found it very difficult to handle the PTSD. I also now realized the unpredictable circumstances that could come with working a service job like this.

SOMETHING DID NOT FEEL RIGHT

— ★ ★ ★ —

As much as I enjoyed my job before this terrible event, I didn't anymore. I knew that a career change would be necessary to move forward.

I was nervous about having to make a change. I also knew it would put a huge burden on my husband to have to pick up the financial slack from me taking such a huge pay cut. I was unsure of how it would work out. I found out though. What I found out was that God's favor is so amazing. When you surrender and make a conscience effort to be more like Jesus and to walk in obedience, he will move mountains and position you in places you never thought you'd get to. It doesn't matter to God what your resume says or if you ever had any experience at all in an area field. God can and will promote and honor your obedience.

After I left that telecommunications company, I started pretty close to the bottom, making $12 per hour. I partnered with a company who was moving a portion of their operations to the Houston area. Over the course of the next five years, I received seven, (did you read that? seven), promotions within three years. By the time God told me to leave that job, my salary had tripled since the day I walked in the door. I could go on and on, telling you story after story, about how God's truth and promises continued to ring true in my life.

But today, I want to challenge you to conduct your own self-check. Do you really believe? Are you willing to trust him and his word, without a shadow of doubt? Are you willing to really surrender all and walk by faith?

> **ARE YOU WILLING TO REALLY SURRENDER ALL AND WALK BY FAITH?**
> — ★ ★ ★ —

It can be a journey to get there. I remember there was a period of time after I rededicated my life to Christ and told God I was all in, that somehow I constantly found myself trying to manipulate my finances with multiple credit cards and payday loans. Some might say I was robbing Peter to pay Paul. Finally, I surrendered all of me, and all of my life, to God. It was then that I received God as Jehovah Jireh, my provider. All I can say to that is, "What a relief!"

Don't get stuck on trying to put God in a box or decoding the mysteries before you decide to believe. Remember, there is so much beauty in simply trusting and submitting without seeing and knowing all. It's called faith.

"God is not a man, that He should lie, or a son of man, that he should repent."
Numbers 23:19

Chapter 3

Christ Within You

We are children of the King and he withholds nothing from us. Yes, we will go through the ebbs and flows of life, but the battle does not seem near as bad when you truly understand the power that is within you.

My First Download

I was standing in my parents' living room staring out of the front window. It was a beautiful, bright sunny day in the country. Suddenly, I saw snapshots in my mind of my older sister's wedding that was scheduled for August of that year. The seat where my brother-in-law's mother was planned to sit had a sign with her name on it and beautiful flowers.

At first, not only did I not know what to think of it, I started wondering if I had seen something on TV and it was coming back to me. Was this a not-so-funny trick that my imagination was playing on me?

After a few days, I realized that I had received my first download via the gift of the spirit of wisdom. Being that I was a young teenager, I was super nervous about calling my older sister to share the details of the download and suggest that the wedding be moved up because Mrs. B would not be there if they didn't. During the conversation, she shared with me that the family had just been informed that Mrs. B had cancer.

I was speechless and in amazement of the power of God and the gifts that we are given. I was so grateful that the Most High chose me to help bring wisdom to the family. I am glad to say that the wedding festivities were moved up and

Mrs. B was there to celebrate the new union, although she did transition later that year. I witnessed and felt such a heaviness of sorrow and pain for the family.

Wholeness After My Father's Transition

As I shared earlier, almost three months after my 17th birthday, my father was killed on his way home from work. Never in a thousand years could I fathom my father's earthly death in a manner that involved him being hit by a car that was being driven by a young lady who was on her way to Bible study. Even though my dad was a paraplegic in a wheelchair, he had beaten the odds and lived a normal life as a father and husband. His transition shook me to my core. I went through so many thoughts and emotions about this, it was like I couldn't see straight anymore.

I was the last one to see him leave the house that morning. For some reason, this fact impressed something deep within me that I could not explain. Why would this make me feel so nuts? Perhaps I wished that I could have stopped him from leaving. But then again, it probably has more to do with the fact that he only went to work that day because he wanted me to have more money for my upcoming trip to Washington, D.C. Yeah, this one was hard to deal with for sure. Add to this that our relationship had just gotten back to a great place after being broken for many years. It was too much for me to take.

I cried and cried; and I screamed and cried; and I screamed and cried some more. I wanted to question God so bad and ask, "Why would you take a Father away from his wife and children?"

After some time of experiencing God as my peace and my comforter, I began to be grateful for the time I had with my earthly father. Through my father's actions, I learned about love and the importance of family. I learned about the value of giving your loved ones their flowers while they are still here. I also learned about entrepreneurship, which has helped me so much in my business life. But learning from my father that there are levels to our relationships with God has been critical for me in understanding the development of my own relationship with God.

Losing my father felt like a well had dried up. Not only was I empty, I was dry and lifeless.

3. Christ Within You

It's strange how when you are young (and sometimes even when you are older), you can take for granted that people are always there for you. No longer would I receive my morning hugs, my life lessons nor our family Bible study. I hadn't realized how foundational these were to my sense of self and safety until they were gone. The more I grieved for not having my father pour into my cup as a young lady, I more I grew to know the Prince of Peace (Jesus) and the Almighty Comforter (Holy Spirit).

> **I WISHED THAT I COULD HAVE STOPPED HIM FROM LEAVING**
>
> — ★ ★ ★ —

They were there both day and night, continually watching over me and holding me, comforting me, even in the deep hours of the night. Slowly, I began to feel wrapped in God's peace and love. Even though my earthly father was not physically there, I had connected with God in a way that was stronger than death. I felt whole again. Wounded, but whole. Suffering, but whole.

The Fire Within

My relationship with God began to get better over the years. My view of him changed. I no longer saw him only as Almighty God. Now I saw and knew him as the Father, my Father. Our relationship grew, just as with natural parents and children.

While children are teenagers, they think they know it all and that parents simply don't understand how it is today. Then many years later, as the child matures and starts behaving as an adult, the relationship is restored. The child no longer sees things as a child, but as an adult who can now relate to their parents.

I began to be transparent with myself and with God. I was no longer making excuses for my shortcomings and childhood issues. I was no longer saying things like, "This was how I was raised," or "This is just how God made me." This is when I became open to understanding the role of the Holy Spirit and the gifts of the Spirit.

I am sure we have all seen men and women of God lay hands on believers for prayer, healing and impartation. Some believers received and some didn't. Some may lay out on the floor or start to dance, while others will return to their seats and say they didn't feel anything. I am so very guilty of being that nonbeliever in church saying, "It doesn't take all that," and "You won't catch me running around or passing out." My older sister would simply smile and say, "One day you will feel the fire," and of course, I would always laugh it off.

God always has a purpose and he always has a way. As I began to be more real with my Heavenly Father, my walls continued to come down. As these walls crumbled, I started to receive more spiritually by being open to all of God. Amazing.

> **I WAS NO LONGER MAKING EXCUSES**
> ★★★

All it took for me to have more of God was for him to have more of me. Someone shared with me that a closed hand cannot receive anything and when you raise yours to God, it's an invitation and offering of submission. The first time that I felt the Holy Spirit, I can only describe the experience as a thick, still, peacefulness that made me want to rest and slowly breathe him in.

While laying there in his presence, my surroundings didn't matter and I didn't care what others thought of me. Just to be and feel that free from others' opinions was a miracle to me, but I was infatuated with this amazing feeling of breath and peace. I can still recall feeling the fire for the first time as if it just happened.

We were at a Watch Night Service at my mother's church in the country. I can recall attending Watch Night Services throughout my childhood and still do as an adult with my own family. Watch Night, also known as Freedom Eve, has long been a part of African American culture. It started on December 31, 1862 as many slaved and freed African American people gathered together in homes and local churches awaiting the Emancipation Proclamation, which had been signed by President Abraham Lincoln, to go into effect on January 1, 1863. Even though those of us in the South didn't get word until years later, hence Juneteenth Celebration, we held onto the tradition of our culture.

Some also consider Watch Night Service as a symbol of offering the first fruit of the New Year using the Georgian calendar. On this particular evening, I was so happy that my entire family was bringing in a new year in the house of God that I had been in a state of worship even before the service. As praise and worship started to flow, I could feel a thickness in the air. Everyone was praising in their own way by singing, dancing, shouting or whatever their

3. Christ Within You

heart and spirit desired. By this time, I was accustomed to experiencing God through a sense of peace and comfort, but little did I know the fire was going to consume me that night.

From a simple touch from the sister in front of me, I felt a sensation in my legs, so I quickly sat down. I had come a long way in my spiritual journey, but I wasn't ready to be the one running around the church or dancing with ushers surrounding me. While sitting there, shaking uncontrollably with my head in my lap, I felt this sensation move throughout my whole body. The only way to describe what I was experiencing is to say that it was like fire shut up in my bones.

It made me feel warm, numb, lightweight, loved and full of joy all at the same time. Once again, the Lord of lords and King of kings had decided to pour more into my cup. I was amazed. Little did I know that experience would be the catalyst to unlocking more gifts of the Spirit for me; especially the gift of discerning spirits. This gift allows one to determine motivation, the presence and activity of demonic spirits and the presence and activities of angelic spirits. This gift has helped me as an intercessor for family, friends, business partners and within fellowship.

It is one thing to know God for ourselves, to quote Scriptures and even to attend church. All too often we can do the "churchy" stuff, but what about being fishers of men? What about being able ministers sharing and empowering others with the knowledge of discipleship?

I am writing this book because I want to help someone connect or reconnect to the ultimate source -- God. Yes, even in the times we are living in, where it's not cool to be submissive to a man or woman, we need to be connected to the Trinity more than ever. You will notice that I am not including a lot of Scripture references and biblical stories because in order to disciple you or help you reconnect to the Most High God, you must first BELIEVE.

Believe that he is alive and real. Believe that God sent his Son to save me and you. Believe that you have to be real with him and desire a true relationship with him. Then you will be open and ready to receive and activate the fire within. Do you believe?

Chapter 4

Praise & Worship

The words "praise" and "worship" are commonly used together in the church; however, throughout my journey, I have learned and experienced true worship and true praise. Even though they compliment each other, they are different and they serve different purposes. We praise God because we admire, respect and appreciate him. We also praise him to show our appreciation for all that he has done, all that he is currently doing and all he has promised that he will do. The Bible makes many references about praising God and why we should. The Book of Psalms is an entire book of praises to God.

The LORD is my strong defender; he is the one who has saved me. He is my God, and I will praise him, my father's God, and I will sing about his greatness.
Exodus 15:2 (GNT)

Enter into his gates with thanksgiving, and into his courts with praise: be thankful unto him, and bless his name.
Psalm 100:4 (KJV)

Worship is reserved only for God. Through worship, we give reverence to the Most High God, putting no other god or idol above him. Worship involves submission and surrender of your entire being. By worshiping in Spirit and truth, one opens the door to become fully aware and connected to the Most High. The art of surrendering helps to open that door. Surrendering welcomes transparency into the relationship with God. Yes, he is God and knows all, but something special happens when we are willing to submit and reveal our dirt, spots and wrinkles. Surrendering has also elevated my ability to repent before and during worship.

Praise and worship are not reserved for the worship experience segment of Sunday service. Praise and worship is much more than this and can and should take place anywhere and at any time. Praising God is often accompanied by music, but it does not have to be so. We praise God with our hearts and our lips.

> **WORSHIP IS RESERVED ONLY FOR GOD**
> ── ★ ★ ★ ──

I do love to praise God with music. It is fun and gets me moving and singing. There is nothing like singing, swaying and clapping to my favorite song with words of love and awe to my God. I often think about how the Bible tells of David singing and dancing until his clothes fell off. David did not care what others thought of him and he was the King. We can read in 2 Samuel 6:21 (NLT), where David retorted to his wife, Michal, "I was dancing before the Lord, who chose me above your father and all his family! He appointed me as the leader of Israel, the people of the Lord, so I celebrate before the Lord." Above all, David wanted God to know that he was thankful for appointing him and returning the ark to the City of David.

I recall attending an evening church service while visiting my older sister in San Marcos, Texas. Her understanding and desire for God had increased while she was away attending college. During this service, I saw her doing the things that we used to sit and watch others do, like shouting, being overcome by the power of the spirit and speaking in her heavenly language. I sat there shaking my head and thinking, "Really? You go off to college and start "catching the Spirit?" As if she had read my thoughts, she leaned over and told me with overwhelming confidence that my day was coming. Of course, I laughed and said "Never! It doesn't take all that." Boy was I wrong.

The more I praised and worshipped in Spirit and truth, by acknowledging the Holy Spirit and the gifts of the Spirit, while accepting God's whole word as truth, the more I began to enjoy and embrace being intimate with God. The more intimate I was with God, the more I experienced the goodness of God and the more intense my worship became. It is a circle of going deeper and enjoying more and is available to anyone who is willing.

These days, tears begin to fall just thinking of the many ways he has brought me through life's trials. God was not only there with me, but he carried me through

4. Praise and Worship

the difficulties of being a teenage mom, losing my father when I was 17, living through verbal abuse, mental struggles, divorce, having a premature baby, my daughter having open heart surgery at 11 months of age, car accidents, and all the rest of life's troubles.

God was there in all of life's wonderful, joyous and great moments too and He lifted me up high when he gave me a husband who really loves me.

I live with a heart of gratitude. I could never give God enough praise and honor to thank him for all that he has done and all that he will do. Praise and worship are for God, but I realize that I need to give it just has much as he desires to receive it. I could be feeling down and out, but after praise and worship, I am replenished and confident in my divine destiny.

Worship aligns me with God. I believe that worship releases the power of God in and upon my life in new and exciting ways. I have received new spiritual gifts and experienced a higher level of sensitivity to the activity of the Spirit.

In 2 Kings 3, the Prophet Elisha was called upon for direction and he asked for a harpist. While the harpist was playing, the hand of the Lord came on Elisha. Elisha understood that entering into a state of worship with music would quickly align him with God so that he could give the men direction according to the Lord. During worship, I have received new tongues, seen things in the Spirit and heard God speak.

I realize that for some, the unknown creates space for fear and hesitation. Some may even be cautious to increase their praise and worship because of past experiences and embedded traditions from youth. I encourage you to remove all of your preconceived ideas of what it means or how it feels to experience God, and especially the Holy Spirit.

WE PRAISE GOD WITH OUR HEARTS AND OUR LIPS.

— ★★★ —

My mother always says that the Holy Spirit is a gentleman. In the words of Joyce Meyer, "The Holy Spirit is a gentleman. He will not force Himself into your life in His fullness uninvited. He will fill you, but only if you ask Him to do so. In Luke 11:13, Jesus promises that God will give the Holy Spirit to those who ask Him. And James 4:2 tells us that the reason we do not have certain things is that we do not ask for them."

During my early years of surrender, I realized that God knows all about me because he created me. Of course! He knows how I am wired and how I think because he made me. So he knows what I need and how much I can handle. God would not allow me to experience him in a way that made me feel uncomfortable. Remember, the Holy Spirit is ready and willing to come into your life and he knows how much you can handle according to your capacity. And I love the fact that as your capacity and understanding grow, he grows with you.

I challenge you to:

- *Make your praise a little louder.*
- *Turn up the intensity of your worship.*
- *Put on your blinders - as if it's only you and God.*
- *Open your heart and love on him.*
- *Invite the Holy Spirit into your life.*
- *Allow him to be a gentleman.*

Chapter 5

Intimacy Through Fasting, Prayer & Giving

Hands down, one of the number one reasons that I contribute to the spiritual growth I have seen in my relationship with God has come from me making conscious sacrifices and fasting.

There is something special that happens when time is set apart to go deeper in any relationship, especially a spiritual one. Everyone knows that in order to move to the next level in a relationship, all parties must be willing to make time commitments in order to commune with each other. I have seen couples that have been together for so many years that they can finish each other's sentences or even communicate with each other without saying a word. The same goes for our relationship with God.

The more time we spend with God, the more we begin to think, speak and act like him. Instead of spending all of our time doing only what we want, if we set aside time to fast and pray with God, our lives will improve on every level. Coming out of a period of intimacy with God makes you feel rejuvenated, loved, encouraged and ready to do whatever you are called to do because you love him just that much.

You don't want to leave out this aspect of your relationship with God. That would be equivalent to a married couple sleeping in separate rooms, agreeing not to be intimate and only communicating via text message. In no time, the relationship will lose its authenticity and you will only stay married for the children or financial stability. Don't love God out of guilt or stability. Love him because you can't imagine life without his love. Love him because you want to grow into a beautiful child of the kingdom that he created you to be.

Contrary to popular belief, fasting is not just what people did in the Old Testament or that believers in the early church did. Even Jesus fasted and was tempted. As disciples of the Kingdom, shouldn't we fast as well because we experience temptation on a daily basis? Fasting increases our endurance so that we can be stretched to our next level of capacity.

We need to practice fasting because we live in a society that promotes a microwave mentality, coupled with selfish tendencies, causing us to not leave enough room for God.

Fasting will also help counteract a huge obsession with food, especially here in the U.S. Everywhere we look, food in excess is being promoted, which leads us to subconsciously making our stomach our king. I was very guilty of falling slave to what some call "King Stomach."

I would wake up thinking about food and coffee. As soon as I got to work, I was thinking about lunch, and then on the way home from work, the main topic of discussion was what's for dinner. King Stomach ruled me and my house for many years. I decided to take my relationship with God to the next level by submitting myself to God and sacrificing things that were dear to me. When I began to do this, my relationship with food began to change.

Fasting Gets Results

As a young teenager and adult, I would try to participate in our church's annual Daniel fast at the beginning of each year. Most of the time, I would fall short and have to restart multiple times within the 21-day period. But no matter how many times I fell off, I would always sense growth in some area of my spiritual life. This continued growth caused me to mature and increased my level of willpower to continue to sacrifice and fast.

I realized that I needed to go into each season of fasting with clear prayers, questions and expectations for God, just like any other area in my life that I wanted to be successful in. God does not want us to come to him with a broad,

5. Intimacy Through Fasting, Prayer & Giving

general request. He wants us to be exact, to be specific and to have enough faith that he is going to do it. I also realized that one of the reasons that we often lack power and authority as Kingdom disciples is because we don't have the discipline to fast, nor do we have the faith that we can complete the fast and bring our true request to the throne.

FASTING INCREASES OUR ENDURANCE

—★★★—

Fasting has changed my life forever because it has unlocked a door in the spiritual realm that not only puts me in a position to receive from God, but my spiritual clarity in hearing and seeing becomes much more focused during each season of fasting. Have you ever heard someone say that they are sensitive to things in the atmosphere? They have entered into another level of intimacy with God, which allows them to operate in the natural and supernatural in greater ways.

Fasting With Prayer Gets Even Better Results

I made a post on social media that stated, "Prayer changes things… If you agree, type Amen." I got so many likes and over 100 comments. The following week I posted that same post only changing the word "Prayer" to "Fasting" and do you know that I didn't get half the amount of likes and comments as the week before. I began to ask myself, "Why is fasting not a major part of every believer's life?" Then I realized that so many of us have been tricked into believing that, "It doesn't take all that."

Why would we fast when we can receive what we desire without it? Where would we get that idea from? There are so many pastors and leaders who do not teach on the power of fasting and prayer together. Unfortunately, I hear many messages of God's favor and prosperity, and while this is true also, it is not equipping the Body of Christ for spiritual warfare.

Now, don't get me wrong, the favor of God is amazing. His favor has the power to appoint one to positions that they are not even qualified and have no experience in. As my mother would say, "Favor is not fair, but it's necessary." Favor is necessary to show believers and non-believers alike how sweet it is to serve the Most High God. And who doesn't like prosperity, living in abundance and the overflow?

FASTING HAS CHANGED MY LIFE FOREVER
— ★ ★ ★ —

But what about applying the practical duties of this walk which will enable believers to activate the power of the Living God within them to work with God in delivering His people who are suffering and bringing others into the Kingdom? What about getting about our Father's business rather than being all about our own? What about it?

In Mark 9, we learn about the boy who had been tormented since childhood. His father took him to the disciples, but they were not able to cast out the mute and deaf tormenting spirit. Jesus returned to the multitude and was able to cast out the demon. While in private, the disciples asked Jesus why they were not able to help the boy and he responded saying, "However, this kind does not go out except by prayer and fasting."

I love this piece of knowledge that Jesus shared. It lets us know that there is another level in the power and authority that we have as followers of Christ. In order to receive it, one only needs to deny himself through fasting and praying. Have you ever been in church or part of a discussion and thought to yourself that there has to be more to this life as a believer?

If we are supposed to model ourselves and our lives according to the life of Jesus, shouldn't we have more supernatural experiences? The answer is a definite YES! Jesus said that supernatural signs would follow the believer. Can you claim that in your life? The gifts and calling of God are without repentance. See Romans 11:29. Another word for repentance here is irrevocable. This means that God will not change his mind about what he has called you to do or take back any gifts he gave you. They are all still there whether or not you have obeyed. Yet, in order to receive them all, it is going to cost you your time and your obedience. Are you willing to pay the price?

Fasting, Prayer & Giving Gets Even Greater Results

We all know that faith without works is dead, and as we see in Matthew 6, Jesus lays down the foundation of three critical practices that each believer should be participating in regularly. Jesus makes it clear that fasting, prayer and giving should be part of our normal Christian life.

5. Intimacy Through Fasting, Prayer & Giving

When we fast, pray and give, we create a three-strand cord. The Bible talks about how a three-strand cord is not easily broken in Ecclesiastes 4:12. Creating that cord unlocks new levels in our spiritual life where we can experience breakthroughs, strongholds being broken, cancellation of demonic plans, healing virtue, spiritual gift development and overflow.

One of the first things that we have to do as believers is to eradicate the F.E.A.R or false evidence appearing real. Attempting to dwell in both fear and faith causes extreme chaos and confusion, which hinders us as believers from getting greater results. We have been given the formula of the three-strand cord; however, there are so many of us believers who don't live the life that God designed for us because of fear.

As we grow with God, just as in any relationship, we desire more. The first cord of fasting helps us get the more that we desire. No matter if it's more understanding, more gifts, more answers, more growth or even more power to resist temptation, fasting will help. Fasting helps get those better results that we are seeking because when you are in a relationship with the Father, there is always another level or layer that he is peeling away as we transition to look more and more like him.

The second cord is prayer. I love the fact that I can talk and commune directly with the Father. No middleman. No veil. No major protocols. We can just talk to God. He is our father and friend and we should be comfortable speaking to him just as to our earthly fathers and friends. God hears our prayers and he answers them. Being able to pray is a privilege, but in some cases, a failure for so many of us Christians. What is easy to do is also easy not to do.

ARE YOU WILLING TO PAY THE PRICE?

Perhaps if we had to put in more work in order to pray then some might hold it at a higher value instead of a " Get Out of Jail" card that we play when we are in a bind and need God's help. The cord of prayer is an invitation to God and it helps bind us to him. God is a jealous, yet just, God. He gives us free-will and the choice to love him back. And that choice makes the cord of prayer so strong and powerful, which in turn creates more understanding regarding the level of intimacy that can be achieved through our relationship with him.

WHAT IS EASY TO DO IS ALSO EASY NOT TO DO

— ★ ★ ★ —

I cannot recall how many times I have heard someone say, "I am not giving my money to the church because I know that the Pastor is going to take it for personal use." I would be wrong if I did not admit that there have been individuals who have misused funds that were given; however, those individuals have to answer to God for their actions. In whatever way others choose to respond to what I give, that does not give me permission to neglect the act of giving and the sowing of seeds. Sowing and reaping is a beautiful thing when it is done out of love and joy.

The Word of God says that the person who gives bountifully will also reap bountifully. Giving (also called sowing) is so much bigger than just money. Money is simply one of the tools that we use to apply the law of sowing and reaping. Many times it is easier to give than it is to receive. Have you noticed that? What do you do with the reaping portion of this law?

We need to start applying the law of receptivity to both sides of sowing and reaping. The law of receptivity states that the key to effective giving is to stay open to receive. Why is it so hard for us to stay open to receive our good and bountiful harvest? For myself, I realized that somewhere along the line I was programmed to believe that giving was good and receiving was not so good. Again, this is not just about money.

So many seeds of pride have been planted and grown into a deep-rooted mindset in some people who can't even accept a compliment or appreciate a gift without feeling awkward or even guilty for not having a compliment to return or a gift to give to the giver. Perhaps it's because it is so easy to believe the lie that we are not deserving of the good. It's a broken mindset that we simply need to fix. It's also a madness of torment that needs to stop. Believe what the Word of God says. I choose to believe that where the Word says that I will "reap bountifully," I will and I am ready to recognize and receive my harvest at all times.

In the book *The Go-Giver*, the two main characters, Pindar and Joe, have a discussion about this law and relate it to life, literally. They relate it to breathing. As I take in a nice big deep breath, it's followed by what? A nice healthy exhale, right? So what is more important, the inhale or the exhale? Neither, right! They are both equally as important! You won't survive if you are only able to exhale or only able to inhale. You must exhale AND inhale to stay alive.

5. Intimacy Through Fasting, Prayer & Giving

Both the giving and the receiving are necessary to your life. What about your heart? Your heart compresses and relaxes. It compresses and relaxes to pump blood through your body. So which is more important, the compression or the relaxing? Again, neither! You can't survive if your heart just compresses or just relaxes. Both are necessary to live. Again, it's the giving and receiving that is necessary to your life.

> **YOU MUST EXHALE AND INHALE TO STAY ALIVE**
> ─ ★ ★ ★ ─

Well, the same goes for all other giving and receiving in the world! In fact, every giving is only possible because there is also a receiving! Choose to be in the flow of life. Be open to receiving good into your life. Bob Burg says, "When you live generously and focus on creating value for others, great value will come to you, suddenly and unexpectedly from unseen places."

Don't miss out on all that God has for you just because you have not established your three-strand cord or your cord is not securely wrapped around your life. A single scarlet cord spared Rahab and her family's lives during the destruction of Jericho.

Just imagine what the three-strand cord of fasting, prayer and giving can do for you and your family.

Chapter 6

The Reason For The Lie

How often do you continue to fellowship with someone who has stolen from your household and family? How often do you remain cordial with someone who has killed your loved ones physically, emotionally or mentally? When was the last time you invited someone into your home to stay for a while even though every time they visited something is destroyed?

Would you remain cool with someone who was a sneaky slider and all they wanted to do, by any means necessary, was keep you out of the will of God? I pray that the answer is no; a resounding no.

As mentioned, we have an enemy who is aiming to steal, kill and destroy us and our lives. Satan knew who I was before I knew. He sees our gifting and anointing, because God has given and made available every tool, talent and resource that we need to succeed.

Some may believe that Satan is this red creature with horns with a mindset of Megatron that hates humans and simply wants to make alliances with some and destroy everyone else. But I like how the Easton's Bible Dictionary defines him, as follows:

Satan: adversary; accuser. When used as a proper name, the Hebrew word so rendered has the article "the adversary" (Job 1:6-12; 2:1-7). In the New Testament it is used as interchangeable with Diabolos, or the devil, and is so used more than thirty times.

He is also called "the dragon," "the old serpent" (Revelation 12:9; 20:2); "the prince of this world" (John 12:31; 14:30); "the prince of the power of the air" (Ephesians 2:2); "the god of this world" (2 Corinthians 4:4); "the spirit that now worketh in the children of disobedience" (Ephesians 2:2).

The distinct personality of Satan and his activity among men are thus obviously recognized. He tempted our Lord in the wilderness (Matthew 4:1-11). He is "Beelzebub, the prince of the devils" (12:24). He is "the constant enemy of God, of Christ, of the divine kingdom, of the followers of Christ, and of all truth; full of falsehood and all malice, and exciting and seducing to evil in every possible way." His power is very great in the world. He is a "roaring lion, seeking whom he may devour" (1 Peter 5:8). Men are said to be "taken captive by him" (2 Timothy 2:26). Christians are warned against his "devices" (2 Corinthians 2:11), and called on to "resist" him (James 4:7).

Christ redeems his people from "him that had the power of death, that is, the devil" (Hebrews 2:14). Satan has the "power of death," not as lord, but simply as executioner.

Now that we have a clear depiction of who Satan is and who he isn't let's discuss that reason for the lie. Some may say he wants your soul or he wants you to worship him or even to control you, but the simple reason for all that he does is DOUBT. He wants you to doubt God and his Word being true in your life.

It is just as he did with Eve in the Garden of Eden. His first words to Eve were, "Has God indeed said," which led her to reconsider what God said to Adam. If a believer began to doubt that God is real, doubt that he is alive, doubt that we have power, or even doubt the Word of God as truth, then Satan has room to come in to steal, kill and destroy.

HE WANTS YOU TO DOUBT GOD

— ★ ★ ★ —

For so many years, I simply existed and lived in fear. I tried to play it safe just in case I transitioned, I would see heaven. I would say things like, "God knows my heart," or "God and I have a special relationship." I usually would use those lines when another believer asked me a question about my relationship with God. I knew I wasn't where I needed to be, but I would say, "I have a good heart for people and I do nice things occasionally," or justify my position with, "I don't go to the clubs anymore and I take care of my family." I lived in fear of dying, so that I failed to live. I never bothered to find out who this God was who is living within me, or anything about His power and His Kingdom, also living in me.

The Lies

Once I realized that the father of lies is nothing but a dog with no new tricks, there were some truths that I needed to rediscover. I had to be willing to go through my healing process into wholeness and my journey to worthiness.

First, I had to become aware of the tricks of the enemy that I would fall for because I would believe them and fall. I found that having a feeling of unworthiness was one of those tricks. Also, comparing myself to others and feeling inadequate, or when I would stop going to church or stay away from other believers (forsaking the fellowship), these were other tricks that I would fall for. I have to say though, that when I would make all these excuses and justifications about my sins and minimize them, the fall would be much harder. I realized I was pacifying sin; or better yet, quieting my sin to the point that there was no guilt or remorse.

I was a shy young girl and over the years my insecurities and flaws caused that shyness to grow into a forest of unworthiness. I believed I was unworthy of being loved, having a great career, thriving in business and friendships (I mean real friends). I worked hard to try to obtain all of these, plus more. But deep down inside, my mountain of unworthiness had always been a distraction prohibiting me from seeing clearly. One must envision themselves at the next level before taking the first step of the journey and that mountain of unworthiness obstructed my view of the future version of me.

Unworthiness is a lie that is used to keep us from operating in our royal Kingdom flow of life. It will subconsciously sabotage your flow. Unworthiness will cause you to question the word and the pure love of God for you. Unworthiness will leave you wondering if you can experience the Holy Spirit. This lie is so powerful that it even makes some believers decrease in faith when they sin after accepting God.

My unworthiness opened the door to self-sabotage in every area of my life, including parenting, relationships, sex, work and fellowship with God. When we take on the lie of our unworthiness, our standards are lowered and

UNWORTHINESS IS A LIE

mediocrity becomes the new norm. Dreams, goals, and aspirations are put aside as we begin to focus on pleasing others. When one is in an unworthy state of mind, self-care is at the bottom of the to-do list.

At one point, I felt so unworthy that I compromised my morals and standards by marrying someone who was unequally yoked. That led to a life and marriage of torment for me. I stayed married to a man who was not being led by God, a man who did not value me as his wife, who cheated numerous times, who fathered a child with his ex while we were together, who verbally and physically abused me and the list goes on and on.

For a season in my life, my unconscious self-doubt opened the door for me to connect with men who I knew were in other relationships and not really available. This only served to increase the lie of my unworthiness and inadequacies and I began to question if I would be worthy even for a real kingdom marriage.

For so many years, I would constantly look to my right and left at other women and their appearance, their homes, their cars, their businesses and feel as if I would never have any of those things because I didn't deserve them or I was less than others or I was totally inadequate on whatever level. I don't know on what level I assumed those other individuals were, I just knew I felt less.

Even though I was working hard to accomplish my goals, I felt as if some things would never go as I wanted. I couldn't even dare to hope that they might. There were even times when I considered my lack of success to be a result of my sinful nature. Once again, it was my fault. I wasn't good enough even for God who claimed to love me. This would only continue my downward spin.

We all have those things that are a part of our individual, sinful nature that most would love to get rid of. Those things we do when immediately afterwards we feel super guilty or get so frustrated because we had the desire to do it in the first place. I like to refer to them as vices and strongholds. God likes to refer to them as sin.

We all have our own vices that lead to sin. One of mine was the spirit of lust, coupled with my daddy issues from my father transitioning when I was 17. Instead of dealing with those spiritual issues, I learned to pacify them. I would not admit that I needed help coping with my father being killed. I needed help

6. The Reason For The Lie

coping from being taken advantage of by an older man as a teenager. I needed help because all my interactions with men allowed me to ignore the void. I just wanted someone to love me for me. I thought that as long as I stayed in a long-term relationship, my issues would not be a problem because I would not be tempted.

My theory worked for a long time until I reconnected with someone from my past on social media. I was never in a relationship with him, but I desired him for years. It turned out that he felt the same way even though nothing ever happened. My lustful nature was reactivated even though I was in a relationship with someone whom I loved deeply. It took everything in me to not give into this lust.

> **GOD LIKES TO REFER TO THEM AS SIN**
> — ★★★ —

As we all know, the enemy will bring everything back in much greater degree to pull us back into a sin we thought we were done with. I realized that even though I did not have a sexual desire for that person my strong desire to be loved and wanted put me in a mindset of lust. Lust is more that sex. Lust can be a desire or string passion for anything. The devil uses triggers of lust that are tied to voids, trauma and pain connected to our souls to easily pull us away from God and our loved ones.

At the end of the day, I realized that sin and desires cannot be pacified, they must be dealt with at the root. You can only give a baby their pacifier for so long before they have to be fed or changed. If you are someone who struggles with cheating, you must get down to the root cause of why you have issues with commitment and exclusiveness. Someone who deals with alcohol abuse cannot simply remove the alcohol from their home because they are going to be tempted while out being social. They must identify the pain and why they want it muted. Someone who deals with the spirit of gluttony cannot simply fast or clean out their pantry because when there is a social gathering or when they feel sad, they will tempted.

They must identify the root cause of the lie.

We all know that John 10:10 tells us that the father of lies, the thief, comes to steal, kill and destroy. How do you think he is going to do that? Do you consider all the ways he can get to you? How about all the ways he can get to someone you love? And maybe even through you. We must recognize that he does it through temptation, fear, chaos, doubt, anger, hurt, greed, loneliness, desire, and confusion. There is no limit to the roads the enemy will take to get to us, to lie, to steal, kill and destroy us.

For a long time, I played into the lie of confusion while I was doubting God and not attending church. I even used the excuse that I had been hurt in church and confused by some of the members' actions not aligning with the little Word of God that I knew. Because I was a teenage mom, I was talked about and made to feel as if I had embarrassed my family. For so many years, I took on and agreed with what others said about me. I had lost my identity and became who they said I was. Slowly, I began to see through the lies after realizing that no matter my relationship status, education level nor job type, no one is going to love me like he does. No one could replace that love, peace and comfort I felt after my father was killed.

I decided to rebuild a real relationship with God and returned to church. I chose a large one where I could be fed and still hide because I didn't want to be hurt again. Eventually, I began to volunteer and my family was called to a smaller start up ministry to continue our growth. We were able to grow more in an intimate setting by spending time with the pastor and eventually taking on leadership roles. Not to imply that we could not have done the same at our old church, but it felt like it was easier to hide and avoid serving because there were already lots of volunteers and staff.

Now that I have shared some of the major lies that I was being fed physically, spiritually and emotionally, I encourage you to do a serious self-evaluation of your own current way of life. You have to be honest with yourself or none of it will really matter. Be willing to face your fears or pain. Use the Word of God as your final answer. The only way to see the lie is to compare it against the truth. Be willing to seek within you that desire for purposeful living that was planted in you by the Holy Spirit. Anything that does not align with God must GO!

It's critical to know that the lies will never cease and they will come in different forms. Remember, the enemy is a deceiver. You don't need to be afraid of the journey or the battle, for God has already given you everything you need for life and for Godliness. See 2 Peter 1:3. It is up to us to activate the Kingdom power that is within us. This will help us to see clearly and to walk in our purpose.

Chapter 7

Self-Care

Most of us have someone who is depending on us for something. Our children, parents, friends, family, teams, partners and even co-workers are counting on us in some way, shape, form or fashion. So, just the thought of self-anything to me would stir up seeds of guilt because I could always be doing something to serve someone else.

It wouldn't matter if it were self-care, self-worth or even self-respect. At some point, in my mind those actions would trick me into feeling that I was selfish, and feeling selfish will take me right into guilt. In my world of church, we were taught the acronym of J.O.Y. JOY means Jesus first, others second and yourself LAST.

Yes, we should be willing servants of the Kingdom. But how effective are we if we are not operating at full efficiency?

This began to take on new meaning to mean when I thought about how before a plane takes off, the flight attendant presents passengers with safety instructions and flight details. There is a part of the presentation that goes over what to do in the event of an incident. The flight attendant confidently informs all passengers that the oxygen mask will drop down and to be sure to put your mask on first before helping others. When I heard this, my first thought was, "Oh my, what mother would take care of herself before making sure her children had their masks on?" But then it clicked.

If we are in extreme circumstances and my children are depending on me to help get them to safety, how helpful would I be if I couldn't breathe?

Self-care does not have to be a long drawn out process each day. Now you will need those full days of recovery here and there, but a collective hour a day can do wonders. It starts with making conscious decisions about what you can and cannot do, along with when you can and cannot commit to tasks. For example: If you have set aside time to pray and meditate in the morning at 8:00 a.m., DO NOT schedule ANYTHING during that time.

Make your self-care time sacred. God has ordained each of us for greatness, but most of us don't sit still long enough to commune with him. How will we know the play if we never make time to talk to the coach?

Once I began to really love myself, setting aside my sacred time became easier. My family began to acknowledge that this was important to me. My children understood that when mommy was in the closet praying or worshiping, then ask dad for help instead of trying to beat the door down while saying, "Mommy, mommy, mommy, mommy, mommy, mommy," until I gave in and opened the door, only to be asked if I had seen their favorite toy.

Once I began to really love myself and take self-care seriously, eating healthy and working out became lifestyle changes instead of a fad. We decided to invest in a home gym because we knew that having to go to the gym was not a realistic option. If you value something enough, you are willing to make sacrifices no matter the cost.

Along this journey of loving myself, I began to love others more genuinely. I was able to see myself, with my faults and all, and yet still love myself beyond measure. There was no guilt or shame, no what ifs or doubts. I experienced confidence in learning and being able to love more. Loving more allowed me to reduce my expectations, which in turn stopped a lot of heartache and frustration. We tend to get so worked up when people don't live up to the expectations that we set for them, but the truth is that they never agreed to our expectations for their life.

My husband says, "Love people where they are, nothing more, nothing less." By being able to do that, I see relationships for what they are. Some are for a season and some for a lifetime. My circle of influence is now filled with people whom I can trust, yet I understand that everyone has a role. Some friends are there just for fun and to take my mind off of my hectic schedule, some are there for encouragement, while others pour into my life spiritually.

7. Self-Care

Taking on the mindset of self-care or essentialism is key to being able to position oneself to walk in purpose or live a purpose-driven life. Unfortunately, bad behavior is praised when we overcommit by putting on our super hero capes trying to do everything and be there for everyone.

Good behavior is frowned upon when we stay true to our boundaries according to the agenda of purpose. Self-care keeps you focused on the main thing, the most important thing. This way you do not continue majoring in the minors and minoring in the majors. When we give all our time and attention to the things that do not even matter, and none to the things that matter the most, we lose.

> "LOVE PEOPLE WHERE THEY ARE, NOTHING MORE, NOTHING LESS."

After I was able to focus on the majors and start my journey to mastering the areas that are priority for me, I began to see life in color again instead of it being a blurry canvas that looked like everyone else's. The grass began to look and smell better and the sun seemed to shine brighter. I know it sounds a little corny and cliché but it's so true. Living a purpose driven life has done wonders for me, my marriage, family, career, business and ministry.

One of the last revelations about self-care is rest. Taking time to rest is extremely vital. I used to think that taking a quick nap or going to bed early would suffice, but I truly needed periods of rest and sabbatical. One of my mentors has shared so much with me about rest. She stated that we all need a winter season and during that season, we are refueled, gain clarity and given new revelations.

> *"Nourishing yourself in a way that helps you blossom in the direction you want to go is attainable, and you are worth the effort."*
> **Deborah Day**

> *"Self-compassion is simply giving the same kindness to ourselves that we would give to others."*
> **Christopher Germer**

> *"Learning to love yourself is like learning to walk—essential, life-changing, and the only way to stand tall."*
> **Vironika Tugaleva**

After indulging in self-care, my worth and value have become clearer than ever. "Never Go on Sale! Never have Commercials!" is one of my daily affirmations. When was the last time you saw a Bentley or Rolls Royce commercial? Never, because the designer knows how much they are worth and valued. If we all knew how precious and priceless we were, then we would not devalue ourselves by staying in relationships, careers and businesses that do not compliment our purpose driven life.

The designers and creators of luxury brands know that their product is enough, just as God created each of us to be enough. Enough to live a purpose-driven life without having to reduce who we are for anyone or anything. I encourage you to set aside time for self-care and notice how priceless you become.

"For you were bought at a price; therefore glorify God in your body and in your spirit, which are God's."
1 Corinthians 6:20 (NKJV)

Chapter 8

Promises Renewed

Spending time with God and reading his Word gives me a renewed sense of self and confidence in knowing whose I am. God has made some amazing promises to each of us to stand on and know that his Word is true. God breathed his own breath into man and gave man life. The Father loves for us, as his children, to give that breath back to him through song, praise, worship and speaking his Word.

God is not a man that he would lie; therefore, his Word will never return to him void. I love saying and praying the Word throughout my day. Even on the days when I am faced with tough decisions, heaviness or I am on an emotional rollercoaster, I find rest, joy and peace in him.

I have listed some of my favorite Scriptures that have helped me throughout this journey of positioning. They remind me of Who I AM and Whose I AM.

"Whereby are given unto us exceeding great and precious promises; that by these ye might be partakers of the divine nature, having escaped the corruption that is in the world."
2 Peter 1:4

"And be not conformed to this world: but be ye transformed by the renewing of your mind, that ye may prove what is that good, and acceptable, and perfect, will of God."
Romans 12:2

"For in him we live, and move, and have our being; as certain also of your own poets have said, For we are also his offspring."
Acts 17:28

*"Then ye shall call upon Me, and ye shall go and
pray unto me, and I will hearken unto you."*
Jeremiah 29:12

"God is our refuge and strength, a very present help in trouble."
Psalm 46:1

*"For sin shall not have dominion over you;
for ye are not under the law, but under grace."*
Romans 6:14

"And let us not be weary in well doing, for in due season we shall reap if we faint not."
Galatians 6:9

*"For God so loved the world, that He gave His only begotten Son, that whosoever
believeth in Him should not perish, but have everlasting life."*
John 3:16

*"Fear not, for I am with thee; be not dismayed, for I am thy God. I will strengthen thee,
yea, I will help thee, yea I will uphold thee with the right hand of My righteousness."*
Isaiah 41:10

*"Be strong and of a good courage, fear not nor be afraid of them; for the Lord thy God,
He it is that doth go with thee, He will not fail thee nor forsake thee."*
Deuteronomy 31:6

*"So that we may boldly say, 'The Lord is my helper;
I will not fear what man shall do unto me."*
Hebrews 13:6

*"Trust in the Lord with all your heart and lean not on your own understanding; in all
your ways submit to him, and he will make your paths straight."*
Proverbs 3:5-6

*"And God is able to bless you abundantly, so that in all things at all times, having all
that you need, you will abound in every good work."*
2 Corinthians 9:8

*"Come to me, all you who are weary and burdened, and I will give you rest. Take my
yoke upon you and learn from me, for I am gentle and humble in heart, and you will
find rest for your souls. For my yoke is easy and my burden is light."*
Matthew 11:28-30

8. Promises Renewed

> *"The thief comes only to steal and kill and destroy;
> I have come that they may have life, and have it to the full."*
> **John 10:10**

> *"For I know the plans I have for you," says the Lord.
> "They are plans for good and not for disaster, to give you a future and a hope."*
> **Jeremiah 29:11**

> *"And this same God who takes care of me will supply all your needs from his glorious
> riches, which have been given to us in Christ Jesus."*
> **Philippians 4:19**

Declarations and affirmations are a key ingredient when you are trying to rid yourself of the old BS and take on a new Belief System in line with God's Word. Romans 10:17 says, "So then faith comes by hearing, and hearing by the word of God." Knowing and hearing God's Word develops our faith in him and his truth. We need faith to inherit the promises of God and to live the best life God planned for us.

Most would be surprised at the outcomes that are manifested when we combine the Word of God and RAS. We all have a RAS (Reticular Activating System) as a part of our brains. The RAS is a very small piece of our brains yet, with the exception of smell, almost all of our senses are connected directly to this bundle of neurons. There are billions of things that our RAS filters out from our brain at any given time because they are irrelevant. Some call the RAS the secret weapon for manifestation, because it is programmed to filter in what we tell it.

> **I FIND REST, JOY AND PEACE IN HIM**
>
>

For example, if you have some unfortunate events happen to you in the morning, then you declare that it is going to be a bad day, do you ever feel as if bad things keep happening throughout the entire day?

Have you ever found yourself saying, "What else can go wrong," and then something else happens? Have you ever gotten a new car and all of a sudden you see that car everywhere you go? Or you learn a new word and somehow you manage to use that word in almost every conversation?

The RAS creates a filter for whatever we focus on. Therefore, if you focus on speaking good news over your life, then the RAS has no choice but to filter in such things, making you a master of manifestation. Will some things happen right away? Yes. Will others take time? Yes. God hears our prayers and declarations as soon as they are made; however, we must be at the capacity to receive them.

If you are praying and declaring $10K blessings and haven't received it, ask yourself what plans you have made for the financial blessings other than seeing it in your bank account. Our level of spiritual maturity and obedience plays a part in when certain provisions and blessings are received so as to be in our best interest and not cause us harm. You will only be able to manifest at your level. Life is a journey with new chapters and levels. We must continue to grow stronger and increase our capacity according to God's purpose and the divine will of God.

8. Promises Renewed

God, I am everything that you say I am.
I am a child of the Most High God.
I am above and not beneath.
I am the lender and not the borrower.
I am debt free.
I speak zero balances and debt cancelation.
I am loved and live to love.
Good things are happening to me.
My spouse is blessed.
My children are blessed.
My family calls me blessed.
I am more than a conqueror.
My house is blessed and protected.
There is nothing impossible with God through me.
I ask for everything that is assigned to me by divine right.
I am complete and lacking nothing.
I rejoice in knowing that I am a child of the King.
I am worthy.
I am beautiful.
I am grateful.
I deserve greatness.
I deserve success.
I am happy, healthy and wise.
I am a friend of God, He calls me friend.
I can do all things through Christ.
No weapon formed against me shall prosper.
In God, I live, move and have my being.
I will not be resistant to my purpose.
I surrender my mind, body and spirit to my divine purpose.
I am faithful.
I am a creator.

Chapter 9

Gratitude & Reflection

> **Gratitude**
>
> noun
>
> grat·i·tude | \ ˈgra-tə-ˌtüd , -ˌtyüd \
>
> **Definition:** the state of being grateful : THANKFULNESS
>
> *According to the Merriam Webster dictionary, gratitude is defined as the state of being grateful: Thankfulness*

Learning how to be and to stay in a state of gratitude has changed how I process life. When you exist in a state of gratitude, the weight of things tends to seem much lighter. The "L's" do not feel like losses. I can see them now as learning opportunities. My gratitude is not only for all the things that God has done, but for his children as well.

I was recently involved in an investment opportunity with partners who I have built strong relationships with over the last year or so. Needless to say, things did not go as planned and relationships were tested. While chatting on the phone with a couple of the investment partners, it was refreshing to be grateful for a situation that most would have felt very discouraged by. I shared with them that I was grateful for what we learned in the midst of chaos and that I did not regret getting involved, because this was a divine lesson that I needed to grow from in order to reach the next level as an entrepreneur.

It is a good feeling to be able to smile in the face of chaos, confusion and disappointment. God has given us the ability to feel emotions, so there should be no guilt for anger, sadness and disappointment. God never promises that we would not suffer. The promise comes with him helping and never leaving us throughout the journey.

One of my favorite Scriptures is James 1:2. "My brethren, count it all joy when you fall into various trials, knowing that the testing of your faith produces patience." Patience is viewed by some as weakness. To the natural eye, giving grace and having patience looks like one is not in control. I find that I give more grace as a result of being in a state of gratitude. Instead of asking why someone made a not-so-smart decision, I pray for them, because who knows what is a part of the cross that each of us is to bear?

The world is filled with hurting people who have mastered masking their pain. The art of masking pain will harden hearts and evoke a state of numbness causing one's judgment to be blurred. We should strive to show love through giving, grace and sharing thankfulness. This will begin to soften hearts and heal pain. Love is an act and not an emotion. The emotions we feel are a result of the acts of love. Living in a state of gratitude will allow you to perform more acts of love. There is an old saying that "hurt people, hurt people." That same principle applies to love, grace and gratitude. People who are loved perform more acts of love for others. People who receive grace are more inclined to give grace. People who live in a state of gratitude are addicted to finding the positive in every situation.

> **Reflection**
>
> re·flec·tion
>
> /rəˈflekSH(ə)n/
>
> noun
>
> 2. serious thought or consideration

9. Gratitude and Reflection

We live in a country that has a social system that focuses on speed and results. How fast can we get from point A to Z? How fast can we turn $10 into $100 and $100 to $1,000? It seems like there is not enough time in the day because our "To Do" lists are rarely, if ever, completed. As a wife and mother, it always felt like there was always something that I could be doing for someone else, which left me with very little time for any personal tasks.

I love how the Bible is the living Word of God. One day I was reading Romans 12:2 (KJV), "And be not conformed to this world: but be ye transformed by the renewing of your mind, that ye may prove what is that good, and acceptable, and perfect, will of God."

I received a new revelation. In order for me not to be conformed to this world and renew my mind, I needed to focus and reflect more.

Daily reflection allows one to examine and evaluate at a micro level. We want to reflect on a micro level so that we do not risk being conformed to this world. There

> **PEOPLE WHO ARE LOVED PERFORM MORE ACTS OF LOVE FOR OTHERS**
> ★★★

have been several times when I thought that I had a situation under control. I did not feel the need to share the details with anyone until I realized that I was in too deep or it became more than I could handle on my own. Looking back, I could have made better decisions and sought help sooner if I had taken that time to evaluate and reflect on the situation sooner.

Having daily reflection time allows you to recognize shifts and changes sooner. When my oldest daughter was born, I would find myself noticing everything about her precious little body. Whether is was a rash or a small scratch when her nails grew or when her first tooth started to come in. Even though I was a teen mom, I wanted to be the best mom to my precious baby girl. I learned to apply that same ideology toward myself. Setting aside reflection time has become a part of my self-care routine and rituals.

During reflection, I evaluate the state of my mind, body and soul, along with the events from that day. As a result of reflection, I have been able to make adjustments in friendships, career, and spiritual growth. It has even helped me build stronger relationships with my inner circle. Before making time to reflect, I overlooked bad habits, disrespect, unhealthy eating, acts of love and the evolution of loved ones. Making time to reflect has made me a better person and catapulted me into a state of gratefulness that has opened new levels and given me access to new frequencies that I did not know existed.

Consistency Chain 90-Day Challenge

- » *Are you ready for more?*
- » *Are you tired of the mundane?*
- » *Are you ready to live a purpose driven life?*
- » *Are ready to walk and live in purpose?*
- » *Are you ready to surrender and allow the Most High to be your GPS (God Positioning System)?*
- » *Do you think that you should be doing more?*
- » *Do you feel that there has to be more to life?*
- » *Do you desire to give more?*
- » *Do you desire to serve more?*
- » *Do you desire to leave a legacy?*

If you answered, "Yes" to any or all of these questions, then it is time for you to build a consistency chain. The consistency chain is created when one is able to commit and remain consistent in completing a task for a predetermined time interval. For example, if someone has a goal to drink more water each day by setting a daily task of intaking at least 40 ounces per day, once the task is complete for the day, I like to put an X on a physical calendar so that I can see the chain grow. Others may want to make note on a digital calendar. The ability to commit on a consistent basis produces astounding results. You will find that consistency is a part of every successful person's formula for success.

Everyone knows the story of the tortoise and hare. We have heard that slow and steady wins the race. Why is it then, that when the gun goes off, so many of us seek to find shortcuts to get us to the finish line faster instead of embracing the process of the race?

Building a consistency chain has allowed me to embrace, enjoy and appreciate the process. Most people want to skip the process and be an overnight success. We assume that successful people found the magic formula to reach goals quicker, stronger and faster. But that could not be farther from the truth. The truth is that those so-called overnight success stories started out with a commitment to consistency and as they went through their process, they grew stronger, faster and it became easier over time.

The road to success and purpose is filled with long nights, early mornings, sacrifices, adjustments, heartaches, pains, disappointments, failures and frustrations. I found that most people, including myself, break our commitments to consistency because the reality of the journey did not match our expectations. We want the results, recognition and compensation before going through the process of being molded into the person who can handle the capacity that comes with success. Money will not solve all of your problems and if you struggle with the process before receiving wealth, how will you handle the load that a wealthy man carries?

To help you on your journey of reflecting, I have created a 90-day reflection journal for both Morning Glory and Evening Reflections. This process has helped me live in a state of gratitude even in very difficult situations. I know it will do the same for you.

Morning Glory

The first hour of the day is vital and crucial to the flow of the rest of the day. I start my day off by identifying things that I am grateful for, prayer, mediation, physical activity, personal development and the review of scheduled tasks for the day so that expectations are set. Waking up a little earlier was ROUGH in the beginning, but now it is second nature and I feel off when I don't have my Morning Glory hour.

The number one principle for repositioning is understanding who God is to us. When we understand that, we also understand that we have to stay connected to him as our source. During the morning glory hour, I submit my spiritual self, along with my physical self, to him by giving him my first fruit of the day. If I stay connected and align myself with God as my source, everything else has no choice but to fall in place.

The physical activity in the morning opens you up for creativity. We are constantly plugging and tuning into others so that we often forget what our own inner voice sounds like. Hormones, such as adrenaline, are released that will keep you moving throughout the morning removing the need for coffee and sugary foods to help get your day started. I sometimes change the order of morning glory rituals because it is more about committing to the process over perfection.

"Authenticity is freedom from the illusion of fear and alignment to the reality of love."
Unknown

Evening Reflection

The evening reflection time is at a much slower pace than the morning glory. The reflection time is spent at the end of the day when all my tasks are complete. Hopefully, my husband and children have been taken care of and now I must make time for self-care. During reflection, I start off in prayer and slowly transition into reviewing the events of the day. I consider what went well and if I faced any obstacles or struggles. I am seeing if there are any outliers or anything that happened that I should revisit and simply make note of for future reference. I typically have my calendar out to glance over so that my expectations are set for the next day.

> *"Learning without reflection is a waste.*
> *Reflection without learning is dangerous."*
> **Confucius**

Morning Glory

Date: _____

I am grateful for:

_____
_____
_____
_____

Prayer Request:

_____
_____
_____
_____

Did I do any physical activity: Yes ☐   No ☐
Did I do any personal development: Yes ☐   No ☐

Notes:

_____
_____
_____
_____

Evening Reflection

Date: _____

Today I learned:

_____
_____
_____
_____

Wins

_____
_____
_____
_____

Obstacles

_____
_____
_____
_____

Notes:

_____
_____
_____
_____

Morning Glory

Date: _____

I am grateful for:

_____
_____
_____
_____

Prayer Request:

_____
_____
_____
_____

Did I do any physical activity: Yes ☐   No ☐
Did I do any personal development: Yes ☐   No ☐

Notes:

_____
_____
_____
_____

Evening Reflection

Date: _____

Today I learned:

_____
_____
_____
_____

Wins

_____
_____
_____

Obstacles

_____
_____
_____
_____

Notes:

_____
_____
_____
_____

Morning Glory

Date: _____

I am grateful for:

_____
_____
_____
_____

Prayer Request:

_____
_____
_____
_____

Did I do any physical activity:　　　Yes ☐　　　No ☐
Did I do any personal development:　Yes ☐　　　No ☐

Notes:

_____
_____
_____
_____

Evening Reflection

Date: _____

Today I learned:

_____
_____
_____
_____

Wins

_____
_____
_____
_____

Obstacles

_____
_____
_____
_____

Notes:

_____
_____
_____
_____

Consistency Chain 90-Day Challenge

Morning Glory

Date: _____

I am grateful for:

_____
_____
_____
_____

Prayer Request:

_____
_____
_____
_____

Did I do any physical activity: Yes ☐   No ☐
Did I do any personal development: Yes ☐   No ☐

Notes:

_____
_____
_____
_____

Evening Reflection

Date: _____

Today I learned:

_____
_____
_____
_____

Wins

_____
_____
_____
_____

Obstacles

_____
_____
_____
_____

Notes:

_____
_____
_____
_____

Morning Glory

Date: _____

I am grateful for:

_____
_____
_____
_____

Prayer Request:

_____
_____
_____
_____

Did I do any physical activity: Yes ☐   No ☐

Did I do any personal development: Yes ☐   No ☐

Notes:

_____
_____
_____
_____

Evening Reflection

Date: _____

Today I learned:

_____
_____
_____
_____

Wins

_____
_____
_____
_____

Obstacles

_____
_____
_____
_____

Notes:

_____
_____
_____
_____

Morning Glory

Date: _____

I am grateful for:

_____
_____
_____
_____

Prayer Request:

_____
_____
_____
_____

Did I do any physical activity: Yes ☐   No ☐
Did I do any personal development: Yes ☐   No ☐

Notes:

_____
_____
_____
_____

Evening Reflection

Date: _____

Today I learned:

_____
_____
_____
_____

Wins

_____
_____
_____
_____

Obstacles

_____
_____
_____
_____

Notes:

_____
_____
_____
_____

Morning Glory

Date: _____

I am grateful for:

_____
_____
_____
_____

Prayer Request:

_____
_____
_____
_____

Did I do any physical activity: Yes ☐   No ☐
Did I do any personal development: Yes ☐   No ☐

Notes:

_____
_____
_____
_____

Evening Reflection

Date: _____

Today I learned:

_____
_____
_____
_____

Wins

_____
_____
_____
_____

Obstacles

_____
_____
_____
_____

Notes:

_____
_____
_____
_____

Morning Glory

Date: _____

I am grateful for:

_____
_____
_____
_____

Prayer Request:

_____
_____
_____
_____

Did I do any physical activity: Yes ☐   No ☐
Did I do any personal development: Yes ☐   No ☐

Notes:

_____
_____
_____
_____

Evening Reflection

Date: _____

Today I learned:

_____
_____
_____
_____

Wins

_____
_____
_____
_____

Obstacles

_____
_____
_____
_____

Notes:

_____
_____
_____
_____

Morning Glory

Date: _____

I am grateful for:

_____
_____
_____
_____

Prayer Request:

_____
_____
_____
_____

Did I do any physical activity: Yes ☐   No ☐

Did I do any personal development: Yes ☐   No ☐

Notes:

_____
_____
_____
_____

Evening Reflection

Date: _____

Today I learned:

_____
_____
_____
_____

Wins

_____
_____
_____

Obstacles

_____
_____
_____
_____

Notes:

_____
_____
_____
_____

Morning Glory

Date: _____

I am grateful for:

_____

_____

_____

_____

Prayer Request:

_____

_____

_____

_____

Did I do any physical activity:　　　Yes ☐　　　No ☐

Did I do any personal development:　Yes ☐　　　No ☐

Notes:

_____

_____

_____

_____

Evening Reflection

Date: _____

Today I learned:

_____
_____
_____
_____

Wins

_____
_____
_____
_____

Obstacles

_____
_____
_____
_____

Notes:

_____
_____
_____
_____

Morning Glory

Date: _____

I am grateful for:

_____
_____
_____
_____

Prayer Request:

_____
_____
_____
_____

Did I do any physical activity: Yes ☐   No ☐
Did I do any personal development: Yes ☐   No ☐

Notes:

_____
_____
_____
_____

Evening Reflection

Date: _____

Today I learned:

_____
_____
_____
_____

Wins

_____
_____
_____
_____

Obstacles

_____
_____
_____
_____

Notes:

_____
_____
_____
_____

Morning Glory

Date: _____

I am grateful for:

_____
_____
_____
_____

Prayer Request:

_____
_____
_____
_____

Did I do any physical activity: Yes ☐   No ☐
Did I do any personal development: Yes ☐   No ☐

Notes:

_____
_____
_____
_____

Evening Reflection

Date: _____

Today I learned:

_____
_____
_____
_____

Wins

_____
_____
_____
_____

Obstacles

_____
_____
_____
_____

Notes:

_____
_____
_____
_____

Morning Glory

Date: _____

I am grateful for:

_____
_____
_____
_____

Prayer Request:

_____
_____
_____
_____

Did I do any physical activity: Yes ☐   No ☐
Did I do any personal development: Yes ☐   No ☐

Notes:

_____
_____
_____
_____

Evening Reflection

Date: _____

Today I learned:

_____
_____
_____
_____

Wins

_____
_____
_____
_____

Obstacles

_____
_____
_____
_____

Notes:

_____
_____
_____
_____

Morning Glory

Date: _____

I am grateful for:

_____
_____
_____
_____

Prayer Request:

_____
_____
_____
_____

Did I do any physical activity: Yes ☐   No ☐
Did I do any personal development: Yes ☐   No ☐

Notes:

_____
_____
_____
_____

Evening Reflection

Date: _____

Today I learned:

_____
_____
_____
_____

Wins

_____
_____
_____
_____

Obstacles

_____
_____
_____
_____

Notes:

_____
_____
_____
_____

Morning Glory

Date: _____

I am grateful for:

_____
_____
_____
_____

Prayer Request:

_____
_____
_____
_____

Did I do any physical activity: Yes ☐   No ☐
Did I do any personal development: Yes ☐   No ☐

Notes:

_____
_____
_____
_____

Evening Reflection

Date: _____

Today I learned:

_____
_____
_____
_____

Wins

_____
_____
_____
_____

Obstacles

_____
_____
_____
_____

Notes:

_____
_____
_____
_____

Morning Glory

Date: _____

I am grateful for:

_____
_____
_____
_____

Prayer Request:

_____
_____
_____
_____

Did I do any physical activity: Yes ☐   No ☐
Did I do any personal development: Yes ☐   No ☐

Notes:

_____
_____
_____
_____

Evening Reflection

Date: _____

Today I learned:

_____
_____
_____
_____

Wins

_____
_____
_____
_____

Obstacles

_____
_____
_____
_____

Notes:

_____
_____
_____
_____

Morning Glory

Date: _____

I am grateful for:

_____
_____
_____
_____

Prayer Request:

_____
_____
_____
_____

Did I do any physical activity: Yes ☐   No ☐
Did I do any personal development: Yes ☐   No ☐

Notes:

_____
_____
_____
_____

Evening Reflection

Date: _____

Today I learned:

_____
_____
_____
_____

Wins

_____
_____
_____
_____

Obstacles

_____
_____
_____
_____

Notes:

_____
_____
_____
_____

Morning Glory

Date: _____

I am grateful for:

_____
_____
_____
_____

Prayer Request:

_____
_____
_____
_____

Did I do any physical activity: Yes ☐   No ☐
Did I do any personal development: Yes ☐   No ☐

Notes:

_____
_____
_____
_____

Evening Reflection

Date: _____

Today I learned:

_____
_____
_____
_____

Wins

_____
_____
_____
_____

Obstacles

_____
_____
_____
_____

Notes:

_____
_____
_____
_____

Morning Glory

Date: _____

I am grateful for:

_____

_____

_____

_____

Prayer Request:

_____

_____

_____

_____

Did I do any physical activity: Yes ☐   No ☐

Did I do any personal development: Yes ☐   No ☐

Notes:

_____

_____

_____

_____

Evening Reflection

Date: _____

Today I learned:

_____
_____
_____
_____

Wins

_____
_____
_____
_____

Obstacles

_____
_____
_____
_____

Notes:

_____
_____
_____
_____

Consistency Chain 90-Day Challenge

Morning Glory

Date: _____

I am grateful for:

_____
_____
_____
_____

Prayer Request:

_____
_____
_____
_____

Did I do any physical activity: Yes ☐   No ☐
Did I do any personal development: Yes ☐   No ☐

Notes:

_____
_____
_____
_____

Evening Reflection

Date: _____

Today I learned:

_____
_____
_____
_____

Wins

_____
_____
_____
_____

Obstacles

_____
_____
_____
_____

Notes:

_____
_____
_____
_____

Morning Glory

Date: _____

I am grateful for:

_____
_____
_____
_____

Prayer Request:

_____
_____
_____
_____

Did I do any physical activity: Yes ☐   No ☐
Did I do any personal development: Yes ☐   No ☐

Notes:

_____
_____
_____
_____

Evening Reflection

Date: _____

Today I learned:

_____
_____
_____
_____

Wins

_____
_____
_____
_____

Obstacles

_____
_____
_____
_____

Notes:

_____
_____
_____
_____

Morning Glory

Date: _____

I am grateful for:

_____
_____
_____
_____

Prayer Request:

_____
_____
_____
_____

Did I do any physical activity:　　Yes ☐　　No ☐
Did I do any personal development:　Yes ☐　　No ☐

Notes:

_____
_____
_____
_____

Evening Reflection

Date: _____

Today I learned:

_____
_____
_____
_____

Wins

_____
_____
_____
_____

Obstacles

_____
_____
_____
_____

Notes:

_____
_____
_____
_____

Morning Glory

Date: _____

I am grateful for:

_____

_____

_____

_____

Prayer Request:

_____

_____

_____

_____

Did I do any physical activity: Yes ☐   No ☐

Did I do any personal development: Yes ☐   No ☐

Notes:

_____

_____

_____

_____

Evening Reflection

Date: _____

Today I learned:

_____
_____
_____
_____

Wins

_____
_____
_____
_____

Obstacles

_____
_____
_____
_____

Notes:

_____
_____
_____
_____

Morning Glory

Date: _____

I am grateful for:

_____
_____
_____
_____

Prayer Request:

_____
_____
_____
_____

Did I do any physical activity: Yes ☐   No ☐
Did I do any personal development: Yes ☐   No ☐

Notes:

_____
_____
_____

Evening Reflection

Date: _____

Today I learned:

_____
_____
_____
_____

Wins

_____
_____
_____
_____

Obstacles

_____
_____
_____
_____

Notes:

_____
_____
_____
_____

Morning Glory

Date: _____

I am grateful for:

_____
_____
_____
_____

Prayer Request:

_____
_____
_____
_____

Did I do any physical activity: Yes ☐   No ☐
Did I do any personal development: Yes ☐   No ☐

Notes:

_____
_____
_____

Evening Reflection

Date: _____

Today I learned:

_____
_____
_____
_____

Wins

_____
_____
_____
_____

Obstacles

_____
_____
_____
_____

Notes:

_____
_____
_____
_____

Morning Glory

Date: _____

I am grateful for:

_____
_____
_____
_____

Prayer Request:

_____
_____
_____
_____

Did I do any physical activity: Yes ☐   No ☐
Did I do any personal development: Yes ☐   No ☐

Notes:

_____
_____
_____
_____

Evening Reflection

Date: _____

Today I learned:

_____
_____
_____
_____

Wins

_____
_____
_____
_____

Obstacles

_____
_____
_____
_____

Notes:

_____
_____
_____
_____

Morning Glory

Date: _____

I am grateful for:

_____

_____

_____

_____

Prayer Request:

_____

_____

_____

_____

Did I do any physical activity: Yes ☐   No ☐

Did I do any personal development: Yes ☐   No ☐

Notes:

_____

_____

_____

_____

Evening Reflection

Date: _____

Today I learned:

_____
_____
_____
_____

Wins

_____
_____
_____
_____

Obstacles

_____
_____
_____
_____

Notes:

_____
_____
_____
_____

Morning Glory

Date: _____

I am grateful for:

_____
_____
_____
_____

Prayer Request:

_____
_____
_____
_____

Did I do any physical activity: Yes ☐   No ☐
Did I do any personal development: Yes ☐   No ☐

Notes:

_____
_____
_____
_____

Evening Reflection

Date: _____

Today I learned:

_____
_____
_____
_____

Wins

_____
_____
_____
_____

Obstacles

_____
_____
_____
_____

Notes:

_____
_____
_____
_____

Morning Glory

Date: _____

I am grateful for:

_____

_____

_____

_____

Prayer Request:

_____

_____

_____

_____

Did I do any physical activity: Yes ☐ No ☐

Did I do any personal development: Yes ☐ No ☐

Notes:

_____

_____

_____

_____

Evening Reflection

Date: _____

Today I learned:

_____
_____
_____
_____

Wins

_____
_____
_____
_____

Obstacles

_____
_____
_____
_____

Notes:

_____
_____
_____
_____

Morning Glory

Date: _____

I am grateful for:

_____
_____
_____
_____

Prayer Request:

_____
_____
_____
_____

Did I do any physical activity: Yes ☐   No ☐
Did I do any personal development: Yes ☐   No ☐

Notes:

_____
_____
_____
_____

Evening Reflection

Date: _____

Today I learned:

_____
_____
_____
_____

Wins

_____
_____
_____
_____

Obstacles

_____
_____
_____
_____

Notes:

_____
_____
_____
_____

Morning Glory

Date: _____

I am grateful for:

_____
_____
_____
_____

Prayer Request:

_____
_____
_____
_____

Did I do any physical activity: Yes ☐   No ☐
Did I do any personal development: Yes ☐   No ☐

Notes:

_____
_____
_____

Evening Reflection

Date: _____

Today I learned:

_____
_____
_____
_____

Wins

_____
_____
_____
_____

Obstacles

_____
_____
_____
_____

Notes:

_____
_____
_____
_____

Morning Glory

Date: _____

I am grateful for:

_____
_____
_____
_____

Prayer Request:

_____
_____
_____
_____

Did I do any physical activity: Yes ☐   No ☐
Did I do any personal development: Yes ☐   No ☐

Notes:

_____
_____
_____
_____

Evening Reflection

Date: _____

Today I learned:

_____
_____
_____
_____

Wins

_____
_____
_____
_____

Obstacles

_____
_____
_____
_____

Notes:

_____
_____
_____
_____

Morning Glory

Date: _____

I am grateful for:

_____
_____
_____
_____

Prayer Request:

_____
_____
_____
_____

Did I do any physical activity: Yes ☐   No ☐
Did I do any personal development: Yes ☐   No ☐

Notes:

_____
_____
_____
_____

Evening Reflection

Date: _____

Today I learned:

_____
_____
_____
_____

Wins

_____
_____
_____
_____

Obstacles

_____
_____
_____
_____

Notes:

_____
_____
_____
_____

Morning Glory

Date: _____

I am grateful for:

_____

_____

_____

_____

Prayer Request:

_____

_____

_____

_____

Did I do any physical activity: Yes ☐   No ☐
Did I do any personal development: Yes ☐   No ☐

Notes:

_____

_____

_____

_____

Evening Reflection

Date: _____

Today I learned:

_____
_____
_____
_____

Wins

_____
_____
_____
_____

Obstacles

_____
_____
_____
_____

Notes:

_____
_____
_____
_____

Morning Glory

Date: _____

I am grateful for:

_____
_____
_____
_____

Prayer Request:

_____
_____
_____
_____

Did I do any physical activity: Yes ☐   No ☐
Did I do any personal development: Yes ☐   No ☐

Notes:

_____
_____
_____
_____

Evening Reflection

Date: _____

Today I learned:

_____
_____
_____
_____

Wins

_____
_____
_____
_____

Obstacles

_____
_____
_____
_____

Notes:

_____
_____
_____
_____

Morning Glory

Date: _____

I am grateful for:

_____
_____
_____
_____

Prayer Request:

_____
_____
_____
_____

Did I do any physical activity: Yes ☐   No ☐
Did I do any personal development: Yes ☐   No ☐

Notes:

_____
_____
_____
_____

Evening Reflection

Date: _____

Today I learned:

_____
_____
_____
_____

Wins

_____
_____
_____
_____

Obstacles

_____
_____
_____
_____

Notes:

_____
_____
_____
_____

Morning Glory

Date: _____

I am grateful for:

_____
_____
_____
_____

Prayer Request:

_____
_____
_____
_____

Did I do any physical activity: Yes ☐   No ☐
Did I do any personal development: Yes ☐   No ☐

Notes:

_____
_____
_____
_____

Evening Reflection

Date: _____

Today I learned:

_____
_____
_____
_____

Wins

_____
_____
_____
_____

Obstacles

_____
_____
_____
_____

Notes:

_____
_____
_____
_____

Morning Glory

Date: _____

I am grateful for:

_____
_____
_____
_____

Prayer Request:

_____
_____
_____
_____

Did I do any physical activity: Yes ☐   No ☐
Did I do any personal development: Yes ☐   No ☐

Notes:

_____
_____
_____
_____

Evening Reflection

Date: _____

Today I learned:

_____
_____
_____
_____

Wins

_____
_____
_____
_____

Obstacles

_____
_____
_____
_____

Notes:

_____
_____
_____
_____

Morning Glory

Date: _____

I am grateful for:

_____
_____
_____
_____

Prayer Request:

_____
_____
_____
_____

Did I do any physical activity: Yes ☐   No ☐
Did I do any personal development: Yes ☐   No ☐

Notes:

_____
_____
_____
_____

Evening Reflection

Date: _____

Today I learned:

_____
_____
_____
_____

Wins

_____
_____
_____
_____

Obstacles

_____
_____
_____
_____

Notes:

_____
_____
_____
_____

Morning Glory

Date: _____

I am grateful for:

_____
_____
_____
_____

Prayer Request:

_____
_____
_____
_____

Did I do any physical activity: Yes ☐   No ☐
Did I do any personal development: Yes ☐   No ☐

Notes:

_____
_____
_____
_____

Evening Reflection

Date: _____

Today I learned:

_____
_____
_____
_____

Wins

_____
_____
_____
_____

Obstacles

_____
_____
_____
_____

Notes:

_____
_____
_____
_____

Morning Glory

Date: _____

I am grateful for:

_____
_____
_____
_____

Prayer Request:

_____
_____
_____
_____

Did I do any physical activity: Yes ☐   No ☐
Did I do any personal development: Yes ☐   No ☐

Notes:

_____
_____
_____
_____

Evening Reflection

Date: _____

Today I learned:

_____
_____
_____
_____

Wins

_____
_____
_____
_____

Obstacles

_____
_____
_____
_____

Notes:

_____
_____
_____
_____

Morning Glory

Date: _____

I am grateful for:

_____
_____
_____
_____

Prayer Request:

_____
_____
_____
_____

Did I do any physical activity: Yes ☐   No ☐
Did I do any personal development: Yes ☐   No ☐

Notes:

_____
_____
_____
_____

Evening Reflection

Date: _____

Today I learned:

_____
_____
_____
_____

Wins

_____
_____
_____
_____

Obstacles

_____
_____
_____
_____

Notes:

_____
_____
_____
_____

Morning Glory

Date: _____

I am grateful for:

_____
_____
_____
_____

Prayer Request:

_____
_____
_____
_____

Did I do any physical activity: Yes ☐   No ☐
Did I do any personal development: Yes ☐   No ☐

Notes:

_____
_____
_____

Evening Reflection

Date: _____

Today I learned:

_____
_____
_____
_____

Wins

_____
_____
_____
_____

Obstacles

_____
_____
_____
_____

Notes:

_____
_____
_____
_____

Morning Glory

Date: _____

I am grateful for:

_____
_____
_____
_____

Prayer Request:

_____
_____
_____
_____

Did I do any physical activity: Yes ☐   No ☐
Did I do any personal development: Yes ☐   No ☐

Notes:

_____
_____
_____
_____

Evening Reflection

Date: _____

Today I learned:

_____
_____
_____
_____

Wins

_____
_____
_____
_____

Obstacles

_____
_____
_____
_____

Notes:

_____
_____
_____
_____

Morning Glory

Date: _____

I am grateful for:

_____
_____
_____
_____

Prayer Request:

_____
_____
_____
_____

Did I do any physical activity: Yes ☐   No ☐
Did I do any personal development: Yes ☐   No ☐

Notes:

_____
_____
_____
_____

Evening Reflection

Date: _____

Today I learned:

_____
_____
_____
_____

Wins

_____
_____
_____
_____

Obstacles

_____
_____
_____
_____

Notes:

_____
_____
_____
_____

Morning Glory

Date: _____

I am grateful for:

_____
_____
_____
_____

Prayer Request:

_____
_____
_____
_____

Did I do any physical activity: Yes ☐   No ☐
Did I do any personal development: Yes ☐   No ☐

Notes:

_____
_____
_____

Evening Reflection

Date: _____

Today I learned:

_____
_____
_____
_____

Wins

_____
_____
_____
_____

Obstacles

_____
_____
_____
_____

Notes:

_____
_____
_____
_____

Morning Glory

Date: _____

I am grateful for:

_____
_____
_____
_____

Prayer Request:

_____
_____
_____
_____

Did I do any physical activity:　　　Yes ☐　　　No ☐
Did I do any personal development:　Yes ☐　　　No ☐

Notes:

_____
_____
_____
_____

Evening Reflection

Date: _____

Today I learned:

_____
_____
_____
_____

Wins

_____
_____
_____
_____

Obstacles

_____
_____
_____
_____

Notes:

_____
_____
_____
_____

Morning Glory

Date: _____

I am grateful for:

_____
_____
_____
_____

Prayer Request:

_____
_____
_____
_____

Did I do any physical activity: Yes ☐   No ☐
Did I do any personal development: Yes ☐   No ☐

Notes:

_____
_____
_____
_____

Evening Reflection

Date: _____

Today I learned:

_____
_____
_____
_____

Wins

_____
_____
_____
_____

Obstacles

_____
_____
_____
_____

Notes:

_____
_____
_____
_____

Morning Glory

Date: _____

I am grateful for:

_____
_____
_____
_____

Prayer Request:

_____
_____
_____
_____

Did I do any physical activity: Yes ☐   No ☐
Did I do any personal development: Yes ☐   No ☐

Notes:

_____
_____
_____
_____

Evening Reflection

Date: _____

Today I learned:

_____
_____
_____
_____

Wins

_____
_____
_____
_____

Obstacles

_____
_____
_____
_____

Notes:

_____
_____
_____
_____

Morning Glory

Date: _____

I am grateful for:

_____

_____

_____

_____

Prayer Request:

_____

_____

_____

_____

Did I do any physical activity: Yes ☐   No ☐

Did I do any personal development: Yes ☐   No ☐

Notes:

_____

_____

_____

_____

Evening Reflection

Date: _____

Today I learned:

_____
_____
_____
_____

Wins

_____
_____
_____
_____

Obstacles

_____
_____
_____
_____

Notes:

_____
_____
_____
_____

Morning Glory

Date: _____

I am grateful for:

_____

_____

_____

_____

Prayer Request:

_____

_____

_____

_____

Did I do any physical activity: Yes ☐   No ☐
Did I do any personal development: Yes ☐   No ☐

Notes:

_____

_____

_____

_____

Evening Reflection

Date: _____

Today I learned:

_____
_____
_____
_____

Wins

_____
_____
_____
_____

Obstacles

_____
_____
_____
_____

Notes:

_____
_____
_____
_____

Morning Glory

Date: _____

I am grateful for:

_____
_____
_____
_____

Prayer Request:

_____
_____
_____
_____

Did I do any physical activity: Yes ☐   No ☐
Did I do any personal development: Yes ☐   No ☐

Notes:

_____
_____
_____
_____

Evening Reflection

Date: _____

Today I learned:

_____
_____
_____
_____

Wins

_____
_____
_____
_____

Obstacles

_____
_____
_____
_____

Notes:

_____
_____
_____
_____

Morning Glory

Date: _____

I am grateful for:

_____
_____
_____
_____

Prayer Request:

_____
_____
_____
_____

Did I do any physical activity: Yes ☐   No ☐
Did I do any personal development: Yes ☐   No ☐

Notes:

_____
_____
_____
_____

Evening Reflection

Date: _____

Today I learned:

_____
_____
_____
_____

Wins

_____
_____
_____
_____

Obstacles

_____
_____
_____
_____

Notes:

_____
_____
_____
_____

Morning Glory

Date: _____

I am grateful for:

_____
_____
_____
_____

Prayer Request:

_____
_____
_____
_____

Did I do any physical activity: Yes ☐   No ☐
Did I do any personal development: Yes ☐   No ☐

Notes:

_____
_____
_____
_____

Evening Reflection

Date: _____

Today I learned:

_____
_____
_____
_____

Wins

_____
_____
_____
_____

Obstacles

_____
_____
_____
_____

Notes:

_____
_____
_____
_____

Morning Glory

Date: _____

I am grateful for:

_____
_____
_____
_____

Prayer Request:

_____
_____
_____
_____

Did I do any physical activity: Yes ☐   No ☐
Did I do any personal development: Yes ☐   No ☐

Notes:

_____
_____
_____
_____

Evening Reflection

Date: _____

Today I learned:

_____
_____
_____
_____

Wins

_____
_____
_____
_____

Obstacles

_____
_____
_____
_____

Notes:

_____
_____
_____
_____

Morning Glory

Date: _____

I am grateful for:

_____
_____
_____
_____

Prayer Request:

_____
_____
_____
_____

Did I do any physical activity: Yes ☐   No ☐
Did I do any personal development: Yes ☐   No ☐

Notes:

_____
_____
_____
_____

Evening Reflection

Date: _____

Today I learned:

_____
_____
_____
_____

Wins

_____
_____
_____
_____

Obstacles

_____
_____
_____
_____

Notes:

_____
_____
_____
_____

Morning Glory

Date: _____

I am grateful for:

_____
_____
_____
_____

Prayer Request:

_____
_____
_____
_____

Did I do any physical activity: Yes ☐   No ☐
Did I do any personal development: Yes ☐   No ☐

Notes:

_____
_____
_____
_____

Evening Reflection

Date: _____

Today I learned:

_____
_____
_____
_____

Wins

_____
_____
_____
_____

Obstacles

_____
_____
_____
_____

Notes:

_____
_____
_____
_____

Morning Glory

Date: _____

I am grateful for:

_____
_____
_____
_____

Prayer Request:

_____
_____
_____
_____

Did I do any physical activity:　　Yes ☐　　No ☐
Did I do any personal development:　Yes ☐　　No ☐

Notes:

_____
_____
_____
_____

Evening Reflection

Date: _____

Today I learned:

_____
_____
_____
_____

Wins

_____
_____
_____
_____

Obstacles

_____
_____
_____
_____

Notes:

_____
_____
_____
_____

Morning Glory

Date: _____

I am grateful for:

_____
_____
_____
_____

Prayer Request:

_____
_____
_____
_____

Did I do any physical activity: Yes ☐   No ☐
Did I do any personal development: Yes ☐   No ☐

Notes:

_____
_____
_____
_____

Evening Reflection

Date: _____

Today I learned:

_____
_____
_____
_____

Wins

_____
_____
_____
_____

Obstacles

_____
_____
_____
_____

Notes:

_____
_____
_____
_____

Morning Glory

Date: _____

I am grateful for:

_____

_____

_____

_____

Prayer Request:

_____

_____

_____

_____

Did I do any physical activity: Yes ☐   No ☐
Did I do any personal development: Yes ☐   No ☐

Notes:

_____

_____

_____

_____

Evening Reflection

Date: _____

Today I learned:

_____
_____
_____
_____

Wins

_____
_____
_____
_____

Obstacles

_____
_____
_____
_____

Notes:

_____
_____
_____
_____

Morning Glory

Date: _____

I am grateful for:

_____
_____
_____
_____

Prayer Request:

_____
_____
_____
_____

Did I do any physical activity:	Yes ☐	No ☐
Did I do any personal development:	Yes ☐	No ☐

Notes:

_____
_____
_____
_____

Evening Reflection

Date: _____

Today I learned:

_____
_____
_____
_____

Wins

_____
_____
_____
_____

Obstacles

_____
_____
_____
_____

Notes:

_____
_____
_____
_____

Morning Glory

Date: _____

I am grateful for:

_____
_____
_____
_____

Prayer Request:

_____
_____
_____
_____

Did I do any physical activity: Yes ☐   No ☐
Did I do any personal development: Yes ☐   No ☐

Notes:

_____
_____
_____
_____

Evening Reflection

Date: _____

Today I learned:

_____
_____
_____
_____

Wins

_____
_____
_____
_____

Obstacles

_____
_____
_____
_____

Notes:

_____
_____
_____
_____

Morning Glory

Date: _____

I am grateful for:

_____
_____
_____
_____

Prayer Request:

_____
_____
_____
_____

Did I do any physical activity: Yes ☐   No ☐
Did I do any personal development: Yes ☐   No ☐

Notes:

_____
_____
_____
_____

Evening Reflection

Date: _____

Today I learned:

_____
_____
_____
_____

Wins

_____
_____
_____
_____

Obstacles

_____
_____
_____
_____

Notes:

_____
_____
_____
_____

Morning Glory

Date: _____

I am grateful for:

_____
_____
_____
_____

Prayer Request:

_____
_____
_____
_____

Did I do any physical activity: Yes ☐ No ☐
Did I do any personal development: Yes ☐ No ☐

Notes:

_____
_____
_____
_____

Evening Reflection

Date: _____

Today I learned:

_____
_____
_____
_____

Wins

_____
_____
_____
_____

Obstacles

_____
_____
_____
_____

Notes:

_____
_____
_____
_____

Morning Glory

Date: _____

I am grateful for:

_____
_____
_____
_____

Prayer Request:

_____
_____
_____
_____

Did I do any physical activity: Yes ☐   No ☐
Did I do any personal development: Yes ☐   No ☐

Notes:

_____
_____
_____
_____

Evening Reflection

Date: _____

Today I learned:

_____
_____
_____
_____

Wins

_____
_____
_____
_____

Obstacles

_____
_____
_____
_____

Notes:

_____
_____
_____
_____

Morning Glory

Date: _____

I am grateful for:

_____
_____
_____
_____

Prayer Request:

_____
_____
_____
_____

Did I do any physical activity: Yes ☐   No ☐
Did I do any personal development: Yes ☐   No ☐

Notes:

_____
_____
_____
_____

Evening Reflection

Date: _____

Today I learned:

_____
_____
_____
_____

Wins

_____
_____
_____
_____

Obstacles

_____
_____
_____
_____

Notes:

_____
_____
_____
_____

Morning Glory

Date: _____

I am grateful for:

_____
_____
_____
_____

Prayer Request:

_____
_____
_____
_____

Did I do any physical activity: Yes ☐   No ☐
Did I do any personal development: Yes ☐   No ☐

Notes:

_____
_____
_____
_____

Evening Reflection

Date: _____

Today I learned:

_____
_____
_____
_____

Wins

_____
_____
_____
_____

Obstacles

_____
_____
_____
_____

Notes:

_____
_____
_____
_____

Morning Glory

Date: _____

I am grateful for:

_____
_____
_____
_____

Prayer Request:

_____
_____
_____
_____

Did I do any physical activity: Yes ☐   No ☐
Did I do any personal development: Yes ☐   No ☐

Notes:

_____
_____
_____
_____

Evening Reflection

Date: _____

Today I learned:

_____
_____
_____
_____

Wins

_____
_____
_____
_____

Obstacles

_____
_____
_____
_____

Notes:

_____
_____
_____
_____

Morning Glory

Date: _____

I am grateful for:

_____
_____
_____
_____

Prayer Request:

_____
_____
_____
_____

Did I do any physical activity: Yes ☐   No ☐

Did I do any personal development: Yes ☐   No ☐

Notes:

_____
_____
_____
_____

Evening Reflection

Date: _____

Today I learned:

_____
_____
_____
_____

Wins

_____
_____
_____
_____

Obstacles

_____
_____
_____
_____

Notes:

_____
_____
_____
_____

Morning Glory

Date: _____

I am grateful for:

_____
_____
_____
_____

Prayer Request:

_____
_____
_____
_____

Did I do any physical activity: Yes ☐   No ☐
Did I do any personal development: Yes ☐   No ☐

Notes:

_____
_____
_____
_____

Evening Reflection

Date: _____

Today I learned:

_____
_____
_____
_____

Wins

_____
_____
_____
_____

Obstacles

_____
_____
_____
_____

Notes:

_____
_____
_____
_____

Morning Glory

Date: _____

I am grateful for:

_____
_____
_____
_____

Prayer Request:

_____
_____
_____
_____

Did I do any physical activity: Yes ☐   No ☐
Did I do any personal development: Yes ☐   No ☐

Notes:

_____
_____
_____
_____

Evening Reflection

Date: _____

Today I learned:

_____
_____
_____
_____

Wins

_____
_____
_____
_____

Obstacles

_____
_____
_____
_____

Notes:

_____
_____
_____
_____

Morning Glory

Date: _____

I am grateful for:

_____
_____
_____
_____

Prayer Request:

_____
_____
_____
_____

Did I do any physical activity: Yes ☐   No ☐
Did I do any personal development: Yes ☐   No ☐

Notes:

_____
_____
_____
_____

Evening Reflection

Date: _____

Today I learned:

_____
_____
_____
_____

Wins

_____
_____
_____
_____

Obstacles

_____
_____
_____
_____

Notes:

_____
_____
_____
_____

Morning Glory

Date: _____

I am grateful for:

_____
_____
_____
_____

Prayer Request:

_____
_____
_____
_____

Did I do any physical activity: Yes ☐   No ☐
Did I do any personal development: Yes ☐   No ☐

Notes:

_____
_____
_____
_____

Evening Reflection

Date: _____

Today I learned:

_____
_____
_____
_____

Wins

_____
_____
_____
_____

Obstacles

_____
_____
_____
_____

Notes:

_____
_____
_____
_____

Morning Glory

Date: _____

I am grateful for:

_____
_____
_____
_____

Prayer Request:

_____
_____
_____
_____

Did I do any physical activity: Yes ☐   No ☐
Did I do any personal development: Yes ☐   No ☐

Notes:

_____
_____
_____
_____

Evening Reflection

Date: _____

Today I learned:

_____
_____
_____
_____

Wins

_____
_____
_____
_____

Obstacles

_____
_____
_____
_____

Notes:

_____
_____
_____
_____

Morning Glory

Date: _____

I am grateful for:

_____

_____

_____

_____

Prayer Request:

_____

_____

_____

_____

Did I do any physical activity: Yes ☐   No ☐

Did I do any personal development: Yes ☐   No ☐

Notes:

_____

_____

_____

_____

Evening Reflection

Date: _____

Today I learned:

_____
_____
_____
_____

Wins

_____
_____
_____
_____

Obstacles

_____
_____
_____
_____

Notes:

_____
_____
_____
_____

Morning Glory

Date: _____

I am grateful for:

_____
_____
_____
_____

Prayer Request:

_____
_____
_____
_____

Did I do any physical activity: Yes ☐   No ☐
Did I do any personal development: Yes ☐   No ☐

Notes:

_____
_____
_____
_____

Evening Reflection

Date: _____

Today I learned:

_____
_____
_____
_____

Wins

_____
_____
_____
_____

Obstacles

_____
_____
_____
_____

Notes:

_____
_____
_____
_____

Morning Glory

Date: _____

I am grateful for:

_____
_____
_____
_____

Prayer Request:

_____
_____
_____
_____

Did I do any physical activity: Yes ☐   No ☐
Did I do any personal development: Yes ☐   No ☐

Notes:

_____
_____
_____
_____

Evening Reflection

Date: _____

Today I learned:

_____
_____
_____
_____

Wins

_____
_____
_____
_____

Obstacles

_____
_____
_____
_____

Notes:

_____
_____
_____
_____

Morning Glory

Date: _____

I am grateful for:

_____
_____
_____
_____

Prayer Request:

_____
_____
_____
_____

Did I do any physical activity: Yes ☐   No ☐
Did I do any personal development: Yes ☐   No ☐

Notes:

_____
_____
_____
_____

Evening Reflection

Date: _____

Today I learned:

_____
_____
_____
_____

Wins

_____
_____
_____
_____

Obstacles

_____
_____
_____
_____

Notes:

_____
_____
_____
_____

Morning Glory

Date: _____

I am grateful for:

_____
_____
_____
_____

Prayer Request:

_____
_____
_____
_____

Did I do any physical activity:	Yes ☐	No ☐
Did I do any personal development:	Yes ☐	No ☐

Notes:

_____
_____
_____
_____

Evening Reflection

Date: _____

Today I learned:

_____
_____
_____
_____

Wins

_____
_____
_____
_____

Obstacles

_____
_____
_____
_____

Notes:

_____
_____
_____
_____

Morning Glory

Date: _____

I am grateful for:

_____
_____
_____
_____

Prayer Request:

_____
_____
_____
_____

Did I do any physical activity: Yes ☐   No ☐
Did I do any personal development: Yes ☐   No ☐

Notes:

_____
_____
_____
_____

Evening Reflection

Date: _____

Today I learned:

_____
_____
_____
_____

Wins

_____
_____
_____
_____

Obstacles

_____
_____
_____
_____

Notes:

_____
_____
_____
_____

Morning Glory

Date: _____

I am grateful for:

_____
_____
_____
_____

Prayer Request:

_____
_____
_____
_____

Did I do any physical activity: Yes ☐   No ☐
Did I do any personal development: Yes ☐   No ☐

Notes:

_____
_____
_____
_____

Evening Reflection

Date: _____

Today I learned:

_____
_____
_____
_____

Wins

_____
_____
_____
_____

Obstacles

_____
_____
_____
_____

Notes:

_____
_____
_____
_____

Morning Glory

Date: _____

I am grateful for:

_____
_____
_____
_____

Prayer Request:

_____
_____
_____
_____

Did I do any physical activity: Yes ☐   No ☐
Did I do any personal development: Yes ☐   No ☐

Notes:

_____
_____
_____

Evening Reflection

Date: _____

Today I learned:

_____
_____
_____
_____

Wins

_____
_____
_____
_____

Obstacles

_____
_____
_____
_____

Notes:

_____
_____
_____
_____

Morning Glory

Date: _____

I am grateful for:

_____
_____
_____
_____

Prayer Request:

_____
_____
_____
_____

Did I do any physical activity: Yes ☐   No ☐
Did I do any personal development: Yes ☐   No ☐

Notes:

_____
_____
_____
_____

Evening Reflection

Date: _____

Today I learned:

_____
_____
_____
_____

Wins

_____
_____
_____
_____

Obstacles

_____
_____
_____
_____

Notes:

_____
_____
_____
_____

Morning Glory

Date: _____

I am grateful for:

_____
_____
_____
_____

Prayer Request:

_____
_____
_____
_____

Did I do any physical activity: Yes ☐   No ☐
Did I do any personal development: Yes ☐   No ☐

Notes:

_____
_____
_____
_____

Evening Reflection

Date: _____

Today I learned:

_____
_____
_____
_____

Wins

_____
_____
_____
_____

Obstacles

_____
_____
_____
_____

Notes:

_____
_____
_____
_____

Morning Glory

Date: _____

I am grateful for:

_____
_____
_____
_____

Prayer Request:

_____
_____
_____
_____

Did I do any physical activity: Yes ☐   No ☐
Did I do any personal development: Yes ☐   No ☐

Notes:

_____
_____
_____
_____

Evening Reflection

Date: _____

Today I learned:

_____
_____
_____
_____

Wins

_____
_____
_____
_____

Obstacles

_____
_____
_____
_____

Notes:

_____
_____
_____
_____

Morning Glory

Date: _____

I am grateful for:

_____
_____
_____
_____

Prayer Request:

_____
_____
_____
_____

Did I do any physical activity: Yes ☐   No ☐
Did I do any personal development: Yes ☐   No ☐

Notes:

_____
_____
_____
_____

Evening Reflection

Date: _____

Today I learned:

_____
_____
_____
_____

Wins

_____
_____
_____
_____

Obstacles

_____
_____
_____
_____

Notes:

_____
_____
_____
_____

Morning Glory

Date: _____

I am grateful for:

_____

_____

_____

_____

Prayer Request:

_____

_____

_____

_____

Did I do any physical activity: Yes ☐   No ☐
Did I do any personal development: Yes ☐   No ☐

Notes:

_____

_____

_____

_____

Evening Reflection

Date: _____

Today I learned:

_____
_____
_____
_____

Wins

_____
_____
_____
_____

Obstacles

_____
_____
_____
_____

Notes:

_____
_____
_____
_____

Morning Glory

Date: _____

I am grateful for:

_____
_____
_____
_____

Prayer Request:

_____
_____
_____
_____

Did I do any physical activity: Yes ☐   No ☐
Did I do any personal development: Yes ☐   No ☐

Notes:

_____
_____
_____
_____

Evening Reflection

Date: _____

Today I learned:

_____
_____
_____
_____

Wins

_____
_____
_____
_____

Obstacles

_____
_____
_____
_____

Notes:

_____
_____
_____
_____

Morning Glory

Date: _____

I am grateful for:

_____
_____
_____
_____

Prayer Request:

_____
_____
_____
_____

Did I do any physical activity: Yes ☐   No ☐
Did I do any personal development: Yes ☐   No ☐

Notes:

_____
_____
_____
_____

Evening Reflection

Date: _____

Today I learned:

_____
_____
_____
_____

Wins

_____
_____
_____
_____

Obstacles

_____
_____
_____
_____

Notes:

_____
_____
_____
_____

Morning Glory

Date: _____

I am grateful for:

_____
_____
_____
_____

Prayer Request:

_____
_____
_____
_____

Did I do any physical activity: Yes ☐   No ☐
Did I do any personal development: Yes ☐   No ☐

Notes:

_____
_____
_____
_____

Evening Reflection

Date: _____

Today I learned:

_____
_____
_____
_____

Wins

_____
_____
_____
_____

Obstacles

_____
_____
_____
_____

Notes:

_____
_____
_____
_____

Made in the USA
Middletown, DE
11 July 2022